YOUR LIFE *is a* JOKE

12 WAYS TO GO FROM HAHA TO AHA!

ADAM CHRISTING

Published by Markin Books.

Library of Congress Cataloging-in Publication Data

Christing, Adam
Your life is a joke: 12 ways to go from haha to aha!
1. Self-Help 2. Personal Growth 3. Humor

ISBN 978-0-9899303-1-4

Printed in the United States of America.
10 9 8 7 6 5 4 3 2 1

DEDICATED to my wife,
all of our children,
siblings, parents, and close friends,
but not to our dog …
I'm not a big pet person.

We don't see things as they are,
we see them as we are.
—Anaïs Nin

CONTENTS

INTRODUCTION

I walked up to the podium so nervous I could taste the fear in my throat. I was about to give the most important speech of my life. I was in 8th grade and shooting to becoming "the Prez" of Granada Jr. High—which in my mind meant mostly becoming more popular and having Susan Morck notice me.

Everything was riding on *this* speech. There were 400 kids in the gym. It felt like 40,000. My name was announced and I started the long walk to the stage. Would I fall flat on my face? How could I get my schoolmates to see me as their next student body CEO? My hands were shaking. I could almost feel the pimples breaking out on my face. Luckily, I had a secret weapon that I had been honing for weeks in front of the bathroom mirror: magic tricks and jokes. I got the magic tricks from my out-of-this-world Uncle Tod. The jokes I picked up like a sponge. And I used lots of them that morning. Years later Jay Leno would tell me that a great comedy routine has lots of LPMs ... laughs per minute. My speech that morning was all LPMs.

I started with a joke I had heard on *The Partridge Family*: "Before I begin, there's something I want to clear up … and that's my complexion."

I made campaign promises: "I will get rid of something evil that has been discovered in the cafeteria … the food." Mr. Grandi was a popular teacher who played basketball with the kids at recess. I made jokes about his hair perm: "Some people have hairdos, Mr. Grandi has a hair don't."

I killed.

My opponent's campaign manager came up to the microphone to speak after I was finished. "Do you want to elect a *clown* for president?" he asked.

The answer from the students who voted was "Yes." I won.

Humor has been my way of getting through the world ever since. I use humor on a daily basis—cracking a joke to ease tension, saying something funny to convince someone of my point of view, or pulling a prank just to get everyone in the room to smile. I also use it professionally. That speech at Granada Jr. High was the start of my career as a stand-up comic. But the reason any of this matters to you is that I believe there are deep lessons we can all learn about life from humor. My 25 years in "the biz" have proven to me that in the simple structure of the humble joke, there are profound truths about perception, reality, our desire to hope for something better for ourselves, and yes, even how to live a meaningful life. I believe that at some level we all think our life is a joke. It's all just a big joke—our money, our work, our relationships. So, the way to a more meaningful life? Don't get more serious about your life. Tell a better joke! That's what this book is all about.

So back to me in middle school. Another pivotal thing happened to me at the ripe old age of 14. I had a crisis of faith. That's young for a kid to experience the dark-night-of-the soul, just as his voice is changing. But I did. My family walked away from the religion I had been raised in. And I became obsessed with the search for the true meaning of life. While my buddies were playing football after school, I was reading Nietzsche and the New Testament and wondering about free will and my place in the universe.

I left 14 behind, thank goodness, but I never stopped asking questions about happiness, fear, relationships, money, spirituality, life, death, and more. Ever since those teenage years I have been on the same quest. "How can I live a more meaningful life?" I have studied the 12 steps, attended Bible college, been mentored by a Navy Seal who is also a Zen Buddhist teacher, worked as a youth pastor, experienced an existential breakthrough via a 3-day weekend training, attended the "Jesus Seminar," participated in the "Money & You" transformation course, worked directly with an NLP hypnotherapist, become a protégé of a self-help master, studied theology and philosophy, become a member of the Ernest Becker Foundation (Becker was the author of not-so-funny Pulitzer Prize winning book, *The Denial of Death*), and become involved with the world hunger humanitarian organization called World Vision.

And ironically, all of the searching has led me right back

to humor, not only as a way to make a living, but as a way of looking at life.

We laugh, we joke, we live.
—Richard Feynman, Nobel-prize-winning physicist

As I continued my quest to answer life's ultimate questions, comedy is how I paid the bills. I have been a professional comedian for 25 years. I've done 3,717 gigs since that 8th grade campaign speech.

These performances have been for a crazy variety of people, including drunken bowlers, Pentecostal preachers, a society of morticians, gang bangers, wealthy financial planners, healthcare workers, surprise birthday party guests, and international sales execs. And those were all at one gig!

It hasn't always been glamorous. One night I performed for a group of insurance agents who had me do my show *inside* of the Boston Aquarium. As I was doing my act, people began to pull phones out to videotape. I felt flattered … until I realized that they were filming two penguins that were behind me mating.

You won't find dirty jokes in this book (with the exception of the previous "Penguins mating" bit), but you'll find lots of laughs. I am the president of *CleanComedians.com*, an entertainment bureau. We provide meeting planners with "Laughter You Can Trust." I still do close to 100 "gigs" a year. Today, I am writing these words a few hours before I will do my comedy magic act at the Disneyland Hotel for a Snap-On Tools awards show. My goal will be to make the audience laugh—a lot—but I also pride myself on getting them to think about life a little bit, too. Because it turns out that laughter isn't silly. It comes from a place that's very close to the heart of who we are.

Like most working entertainers, I travel a lot. I have performed in Canada, Europe, and in 49 of the 50 U.S. States … including China.

I have spent a whole lot of time on the road, but I have spent my entire life *on the road to find out.* The questions I asked were large and small. What makes people laugh? What makes them cry? How do we become who we were meant to be? Are there secrets to finding purpose and creating a more meaningful life? And who books a comedy show in an aquarium? In this book, I will use what I know about making 'em laugh to show you how you can change your set-up, overcome your setbacks, and seize the power of surprise so that *you can rethink the story of your life and tell a better joke.*

This book will help you "get it." I'll let you in on the secrets of telling great jokes, tell you some crazy show biz stories, and share some of the real-life events that have helped me laugh it UP. I will give you 12 meaningful life-lessons I have learned on stage, through financial disaster, during and after a divorce, while accidentally setting fire to a stage, being a dad of four kids, and reading every self-help/spirituality/philosophy/

success book I could get my hands on. We'll look at my quest (and yours) for the answers to life's ultimate questions. Before we are done, I will tell you how, on one particular day, out of all of the billions of people on earth, I actually received "The Meaning of Life" from a nice lady in Florida.

What happens when you laugh is this: You experience a sudden shift in perspective. We are going to turn the Ha Ha's of joke telling into some Aha's! for life changing. I want you to participate with me. My first spiritual mentor, Frank Rodriguez, once told me, "When you mark in a book, a book marks in you." This makes browsing at the library very expensive for me—I have to purchase the books I borrow.

So write in these pages. Get your reactions down. Argue with me. Put stars next to your key insights. If you are reading this on an iPad or other mobile device, highlight away. I promise that if you read *Your Life is a Joke* and ponder the questions at the end of each chapter, you will begin to laugh … for a change.

And Susan Morck, if by any chance you're reading this—I'm sorry, it's too late. I've moved on.

1

YOUR LIFE IS A JOKE

He's turned his life around. He used to be depressed and miserable. Now he's miserable and depressed.
—David Frost

Your life is a joke.

Don't get depressed about it, mine is too! And I don't mean that people are laughing at your despair and slapping their knees in glee over your mistakes, or that a divine being created you as the punch line in a cosmic laugh-fest—although there are times when all of that feels like it is actually true. I mean that your life is a story that shares all the basic elements of a joke—a set-up, some setbacks, and a surprise that gets you to see things in a brand-new light. In order to help you understand how you can play with these elements to your advantage, I'm going to let you in on some of the secrets of the joke-telling craft.

I learned these secrets when I was nine years old from a pitchman magician behind the counter of a dusty magic shop called Circus City in Buena Park, California. This guy was making little sponge bunnies disappear, invisibly fly through the air, and even multiply. It looked like real magic. I had to know how to do it and so I bought the trick. Three things immediately happened:

1. The illusion vanished because now I knew how it worked.
2. I realized that simply knowing the trick didn't make it easy to perform. Creating magic wasn't as easy at looked, and, in fact, it took hours of practice to master the "miracle."
3. I had to learn to live with the shame that I had just spent my hard-earned cash on "sponge bunnies."

Laughter is magic

The other night I performed this same sponge bunny trick for some sales people at a posh 5-star resort. This is 40 years after I gave my two dollars to that guy at Circus City, and 40 years of practicing. I have to say, I'm pretty good at it now.

My audience screamed with delight. It was almost embarrassing. They were blown away. My immediate reaction was that those sales people didn't get out very often, but to them it looked like real magic. At nine years old I lost the illusion of magic, but I gained a love for helping other people see magic (plus the uncanny ability to embarrass my kids when they hit the tween years). That's what I'm going to help you do right now: see the magic in your life.

This may sound ridiculous. Some comedy guy has the secret to a better life? Think about how many times in your life you've said, "This is a joke!" or "Are you *kidding* me?" It makes an odd kind of sense that someone who knows how to get people to laugh knows something about how to get them to be truly happy. And I love a world where it's not the scientists, the presidents, the directors, the Big Cheeses, who have the answers. It's the old magician at Circus City. It's me. *So listen up.* I'm going to tell you some things about comedy, some things about magic and some things about life. I'm going to let you in on the secret to a more meaningful life and it all starts with … a joke.

A man goes in to see a therapist. He's miserable. He's depressed. The therapist asks him to sit down. "What's the problem?" "Not sure I can go on like this anymore," the man replies. "I'm *so* down. Life just seems pointless and depressing." The therapist thinks for a minute. "I know! You need to laugh. Laughter is the best medicine. And guess what? There's a circus in town. My family just went. The clown is hysterical. He'll make you laugh, you'll forget your troubles, and you'll feel so much better. You've got to see this clown perform." The man stares at the therapist and says, "I am the clown."

For years, I felt just like that patient ... the clown. I could make others laugh, but I felt like the joke was on me. In 1996, I was booked for an interview and photo shoot for *Success Magazine*. They wanted to talk about how I was laughing my way to the bank. The reporter and photographer were coming to my office at 10:00 a.m. I was prepping my staff about what to say and what not to say. I was hoping no one would find out that I was completely out of money, buried in debt, and on my way to a devastating divorce. At that point, working in the circus would have been a step up.

You're thinking: *This is the guy who's going to help make my life more fulfilling?* The answer is yes. There's a mess behind every messenger. Behind every master, there's a disaster. So here we go.

Laughter is *not* the best medicine

Comedy is a funny business. For the last 25 years I've worked with more than 200 different comics and entertainers. Many of them are the most miserable and depressed people you'll ever meet. So, I've got good news, and I've got bad news for you. First the bad news: Laughter is *not* the best medicine. Think about it. If you fell off a ladder, cracked your skull open and landed in the emergency room, you wouldn't want the doctor to say, "Hey, this doesn't look good at all. You're losing a lot of blood. Fortunately, I've got a joke for you."

Humor is not always a healing thing. Sometimes comedy is cruelty cloaked in fun. If you picked up this book thinking it was all about the medicinal benefits of humor, you've got the wrong book. (*I will guarantee you this*: If you decide to return this book, I will happily charge you *twice* the purchase price.) There are dozens of books about humor and a healthy heart. Most of them will put you right to sleep—which is probably how they make you feel better.

The good news: Understanding the disruptive and surprising power of humor can help you break patterns in your life, experience a major shift in thinking, and help you rewrite the story of you. So what is the source of humor and how can knowing the structure of a joke help you? Let's start by looking at the word humor. It's the same root we find for the word human. It comes from the root "humus" which means ground or earth. So our humanity is the starting point for laughter. It's also a tasty spread to put on pita bread.

Understanding how a joke works will help you figure out how your life works. And why sometimes it doesn't. *It all starts with the set-up.* You can't have a great ending to a joke (or results in your life) until you have a really good set-up.

Trust me. The first thing the audience hears about

me before I hit the stage—*or how my host sets me up*—affects everything. If the emcee is a pro, he'll set me up real good with an introduction like: "He's been featured on more than 100 radio and TV shows. Please join me in welcoming … Adam Christing." But sometimes the event host turns out to be the company's resident wannabe comedian. He wants to be the star of the show at my expense. I'll get an introduction like this: "Okay. Let me tell you about this entertainer we hired. He's been outstanding in New York. He's been outstanding in Los Angeles. Right now, he's out standing in the men's room waiting to come on. So here he is … Adam Christing." The fact that I still come out smiling and shake the obnoxious host's hand proves that I have some acting ability.

Let me introduce you …

The toughest intro I ever had to follow was at an event for Southern California Edison. They are one of the largest electricity companies in the world. But this was a small meeting. It was a morning gig. There were about 100 macho-looking linemen sitting in a workshop they clearly did not want to attend. Performing comedy, in the morning, for a business, is like waking a stranger up from a deep sleep and saying, "Hey, let's go jogging!" The mood in the room was tense.

The company was asking these employees to contribute their money to a charity drive—just as the organization was about to announce another round of layoffs. Which is another secret of comedy: great timing.

I didn't want to take any chances with this introduction. I handed the event host a 3 x 5 card that simply said: INTRO: "Please welcome to the stage our special guest Adam Christing."

But the man ignored my script. "Hi guys, before I bring up the comedian, I have to share some difficult news. You all may have heard that our friend Bob Jensen, our wonderful senior manager of the last 25 years, was in an auto accident Friday. He was in critical condition over at St. Joseph's hospital, and I just received word that he didn't make it. Services will be held this Thursday at 2 pm. And now … Please welcome to the stage our special guest, Adam Christing."

At that moment something very important flashed before my eyes ... my paycheck. Actually, I felt horrible as a dozen thoughts ran through my brain: should I acknowledge the news that was just announced? Should I pretend it didn't happen? Should I run?

I walked onto the platform just as the wave of shock and sadness rolled over the group. Some of these tough guys started crying. Everybody was looking up at me, hoping I would say something profound. It hit me hard.

I had the microphone. I was in a position to help these people deal with pain, fear, death, and the meaning of life, and so I did the only thing I knew how to do: I used humor. That morning, I told some jokes and got the audience laughing, but what I was really doing was playing the role of minister, philosopher, life coach, and inspirational speaker. I had to change my set-up that day. By listening to the pain my audience was feeling, I was able to tune in to what they really needed—to feel connected.

I'm guessing your life feels painful and disconnected in places, too. I will show you how to change your set-up so that you get a different payoff.

Have you heard the one about ...

Have you noticed how every joke starts off with a set-up about a human being or two? Have you heard the one about a priest, a rabbi, and a nun who walk into a bar? The bartender says, "What is this? Some kind of a joke?" A joke always begins with a person and a premise. Comedians call the premise a "set-up." Some of the all-time great comedians have had the most memorable set-ups. Rodney Dangerfield's premise was, "I don't get no respect!" He looked and dressed the part. Everything he said flowed from his no-respect set-up.

Once he hit you with that opening, the punch lines came naturally. Here are a few timeless Rodney Dangerfield lines that flow from his premise:

I don't get no respect! ...

I'm so ugly ... my mother had morning sickness ...
after I was born.

My wife made me join a bridge club.
I jump off next Tuesday.

On Halloween, the parents sent their
kids out looking like me.

Rodney's premise led directly to his punch lines. Rodney didn't rely on observational humor, improv sketches, or slapstick. He basically told variations of the same joke over and over.

Guess what? You do the same thing. Have you recognized that you keep experiencing the same kinds of problems, the same frustrations, and ... if you're honest about it, the same story over and over again? It's because *you've been set-up*. Sometime in your life—think hard about it, and you may even remember when the set-up set in for you—you decided that your life was based on a specific idea about you. It probably wasn't "I don't get no respect!" It might have been:

Nothing works out for me.

People love to take advantage of me.

I'm not pretty like the other girls ... but I'm bright.

To get approval, I have to hide my feelings.

I may not be smart, handsome or a great athlete, but I have sponge bunnies!

We looked at the word "humor" earlier. Here's another word to chew on: "Set." Notice how it's generally used? Things "set" in. We "set" the table. The stage is "set." We're all "set." Once your *personal paradigm*—your unique "set"-up—gets locked into place, it determines the way you see everything.

You probably didn't even know it, but you have built your entire life on an opening line. Which one? That's for you to discover. But you can change that set-up. Hey, if Eddie Murphy can go from being *Raw* on HBO to being the lovable "Donkey" in *Shrek*, you can redefine your character, too.

Set me free, why don't you?

You are locked in your *prism* from the inside. When you get a new set of glasses with a different premise, you WILL get a different punch line. Here's an example: "The Most Interesting Man in the World" is the focus of a number of funny and wildly popular Dos Equis beer commercials. Watch how a premise totally different from Rodney Dangerfield's leads to radically different conclusions—and a different feeling completely. Here's the set-up:

"He's the most interesting man in the world ..."

His shirts never wrinkle.

If he were to mail a letter without postage, it would still get there.

The police often question him ... just because they find him interesting.

You've been set up

See it? The set-up frames what follows. This is equally true in the story of your life. You've been set-up. If you see yourself as "heavy set," do you really think there's a new diet that will ever make you feel thin? Your set-up makes all the difference. So answer this: What is the premise of your life? First recognize it. Then, if you don't like it, change it. This can redefine your whole experience of life. But like a good joke, you have to believe what you are saying.

I was in front of an audience once and told the life stories of two different men. I hit the highlights for each one in 60 seconds, as follows:

Man #1: Problem after problem

- He got a rare stomach disease when he was a young child.
- He was hospitalized with pneumonia as a high school student. His sister has M.S., and his daughter was diagnosed with scoliosis.
- He lost his house to foreclosure before the big recession hit.
- He went through a traumatic divorce and had to spend $60,000 to get co-custody of his kids.
- He suffers from depression.

Man #2: Blessing after blessing

- He grew up in a nice neighborhood with wonderful parents who loved him.
- He won $1,000 from a radio station when he was a kid. A few weeks later he won a new stereo. Then he won a new 10-speed bicycle in a drawing.
- He has lived the life of his dreams and since school has never had to work a "real job."
- He spends his time reading, and people pay him to say what he thinks.
- He feels like a walking, talking Thank You card.

After sharing these two stories. I told the audience something that shocked them. Both of those men are me. *I can tell either story* (and plenty of other ones) *about myself based on how I construct my set-up*. It depends on how I decide to look at things. The same is true for you. You can reset your set-up and get a whole new personal paradigm. The change can feel magical. Like getting a brand new name. Ever hear about a boy in Hibbing, Minnesota named Bobby Zimmerman? He changed his set-up and decided to become Bob Dylan.

> *You call yourself what you want to call yourself.*
> *This is the land of the free.*
> —Bob Dylan

Here's another example: A boy named Ehrich Weiss was the son of a rabbi. He was supposed to follow in his father's footsteps, but he wanted to be in show business. He wasn't sewing sequins on his yarmulke, but he wanted it real bad. How does a kid whose family is from Budapest, Hungary who then moves to tiny Appleton, Wisconsin, become one of the most famous entertainers in U.S. History? He changed his set-up.

Young Ehrich Weiss read a book about a great magician. He wanted his life to be more like the famous magician's life. Somehow he heard the crazy idea that if he added the letter "I" to a word, it meant "to become even more like that thing."

Ehrich wanted to become more like the famous French magician named Robert Houdin. Ehrich added an "I" to Houdin and changed his name to Houdini. The first major illusion he performed was fittingly called Metamorphosis. Ehrich never looked back. He saw himself as Houdini. He became Houdini. *That new set-up framed the rest of his life*. Houdini became an international star. He died in 1926, but his name is still famous today. Houdini escaped from handcuffs, straight jackets, even a Chinese Water Torture Cell. But his first escape was when he released himself from a life he didn't want. *He changed his life by changing the story he told himself about himself. And it all started with the letter "I."*

You don't have to be a magician (or a comedian) to transform your life. But you have to realize that your life IS a joke. And a joke is a story. And every story begins with a set-up. What's your set-up going to be?

At this point, you have a decision to make. You can:

• Go out and buy yourself some sponge bunnies and practice for 40 years.

• Add an "I" to your favorite entertainer's name and attempt to develop a more powerful career than they have enjoyed. Or ...

• Listen to me, identify the premise that has become the set-up for your life, and choose a new path. It's your choice (but trust me, my way is much easier).

Go ahead, give it a shot. Because currently there's very little demand for an actor named Brad Pitti.

AHA! Lesson #1

Change your premise... change your punch line.

Questions to ask yourself in the dead of night or on a flight to Cleveland:

- What is the "set-up" that governs your life?
- What is the point of view that makes you ... *you*?
- Do you like your personal paradigm? Does it make you feel trapped or transformed?
- Do you want to change your set-up?
- What new set-up would allow you to see yourself as the person you really are (or want to become)?

2

YOUR PERSPECTIVE IS A JOKE

When you change the way you look at things,
the things you look at change.
—The Tao

A blind man walks into a department store. He takes his dog by the leash and starts spinning it in circles above his head. The clerk says, “Sir! Can I help you? The blind man says, “Oh no. I’m just looking.”

ATTENTION WALMART SHOPPERS: It’s not *what* you see in your life, it’s *how* you see it that makes all the difference. Your experience of life comes from the way you perceive things. How do you look at the world? How do you see other people?

Here's another joke to illustrate this point, since we're on a bit of a roll now:

A man has a massive heart attack. His wife rushes him to the emergency room. The doctor looks worried after he examines the husband. He pulls the man's wife aside and tells her, "To be honest with you, I don't like the looks of your husband at all." The wife says, "I don't, either. But he's a good provider, and he plays with the kids."

You may have a vision problem. You may be stuck, seeing yourself, your life, and your relationships through a distorted lens. It's time to get a new lens on life. Remember when we talked about the word "set"? Well, look at the word *mindset*. Notice that it has the word "set" in it. You "set" a cast, you "set" concrete, and sometimes you "set" things in stone. Once your personal life lens has been set up, your life experience gets narrowed into a particular focus. You have gotten used to seeing things a certain way, and you think that's how they are.

I see what you mean

Like the man who accidentally fell into the contact lens machine (he made a spectacle of himself), you have made a spectacle of yourself. You don't see things as they are. You see things as *you* are. Forgive me for a moment if I sound like

Dr. Seuss but …Your point of view is the thing that makes you … *you*. We call ourselves human beings. We're busy being and doing. Let me add to that. You are also a *human seeing*. And *what you see is what you get.* If you don't like what you've been getting, you must change the way you LOOK at things. You need a new set of glasses. Truth is, there's not much you can change about life. But *you can change the way you see it*—and that changes everything.

Disney World opened in 1974. Walt Disney had already been dead seven years. On opening day, a tour guide was excitedly giving Mrs. Disney, Walt's widow, a tour of the magnificent theme park. He said, "Mrs. Disney, "Isn't it marvelous! I wish Mr. Disney could have seen it." Mrs. Disney answered: "He did …"

Millions of people have enjoyed Disney World. And it's all because of what Walt Disney saw in his mind's eye. Albert Einstein said, "Imagination is more important than knowledge." (Which, by the way, may explain Einstein's imaginative hairstyle).

I learned the lesson about imagination for myself when I was eight years old. I was in the second grade, and every afternoon our wonderful teacher would take us outside and have us run a giant lap around the baseball field. And every day the same thing would happen. A little boy named Robert would finish the race far ahead of anyone else. One day—and I don't know why—it just dawned on me what was going on. I noticed that some kids saw themselves as slow, and they were fine finishing last. Some of the boys and girls saw themselves as average runners, and they finished in the middle.

Right then, I vividly saw and felt myself as the leader of our running pack. I pictured myself running out ahead of Robert. And I felt it. I could do that … that's me. And I did. From that day forward, I finished in first place, and Robert ran in second. From then on, I was considered the fastest kid in my grade. What happened? Did I take a seminar about running faster? No. I changed my inner perception about what I could do. I saw it clearly and then lived it.

How do you look?

Important note: I saw it *before* the other kids saw me do it. Too often we wait for other people to change their perceptions of us before we change how we see ourselves. One of the all-time great motivational speakers and authors, Dale Carnegie, who wrote *How to Win Friends and Influence People,* was once asked why he could sell so much. Carnegie said, "Because *I'm* sold." The toughest "sale" you ever make is the one you make to yourself.

When I was twenty-one and considering whether I could make a living as a full-time comedian, I asked my college speech professor, Todd Lewis, "Do you think I have what it takes to do comedy for a living?" His answer was a turning point in my life. He said, "It doesn't matter whether *I* think you can make it. What matters is whether *you* do."

Did you ever see the classic movie *Godfather 2?* There's a powerful scene where the young godfather, played by Robert De Niro, is fed up with being harassed by the bully mob leader who controls everything in town.

Suddenly, it hits him. "They got guns. We got guns." That simple realization, an "AHA!" moment, transforms his life. The soon-to-be godfather has an instant shift in his perception—like what happens when you suddenly get a joke. He sees that he can take power the same way the current bully did—by just taking it. He anoints himself—at that very second—as the new godfather. And it worked, he saw himself as the new mob boss and then everybody started seeing him that way. That is, until *Godfather 3* where everybody started saying, "I wish they'd stopped at 2."

The idea behind *Your Life is a Joke* centers on how a joke can instantly change your perception. You hear the set-up, experience the setback, then you get the punch line. And, *boom.* A new twist, a new perspective, flashes into your mind. So your perspective matters when it comes to laughter and life. Big time. But don't get me wrong. The word reality has *real* in it for a reason. I am not a moral relativist. My friend Enrique Enriquez (you read that right) once told me, "A relativist is someone who has never had his wallet stolen." The point is this: We tend to reside, not in what happens to us, but in our stories about what happens.

I've always thought that a big laugh is a really loud noise from the soul saying, "Ain't that the truth."
—Quincy Jones

You've heard the saying, "If you keep doing what you've been doing, you'll keep getting what you've been getting." It's true. And it's also true that if you keep seeing life the way you are seeing it, you'll keeping experiencing the same stuff, the same circumstances, and the same old life.

Famous comedians all have great "hooks." Jack Benny was the cheapskate. Jerry Seinfeld had a whole show about nothing. Lucille Ball was always getting into trouble. You have a hook, too. Somewhere along the way, you got hooked into a point of view. You need to identify your personal paradigm before you can change it.

Here are 5 ways to spot your *how-you-look* hook:

1) What do you find yourself saying a lot? Do you ever repeat phrases like: "I never win" or "things never work out for me"?

2) What do you see that upsets you most? You may discover that what ticks you off is actually what makes you tick.

3) How do other people describe you? Have you noticed that people say things like, "You are always apologizing for

yourself." Or "You always have to get your own way." Face it. There is no secret conspiracy. People are not meeting in private to define you. You wear your way of seeing life like a strong perfume.

4) How do you explain the way life works? Do you find yourself saying things like, "Well, she got what she had coming." Or "That always happens to *me*." The way you describe life is really just the way you see yourself.

5) What words come out of your mouth when things go your way? Is your response: "Finally, something worked out." Or do you say things like, "I'm on a roll!" The way you see things when times are really good (or really bad) says a lot about who you feel you are at your core.

See for yourself

Here's a joke that illustrates how *what you see is what you get.*

Bob was with his buddies Mike and Brad at the beach. They were walking along, talking about their troubles. Suddenly one of them stubbed his foot on a bottle. You guessed it. A genie popped out. She said, "I will grant each of you one wish." Mike went first: "I wish I was in Las Vegas winning thousands of dollars at the blackjack table with a drink in my hand." Boom. He was gone. His wish had come true. Brad was excited. He said, "Okay, I'm next. I wish I was on a deserted island with the most beautiful woman in the world!" Bam! He was gone. The genie told Bob, "Well, you now get the third wish. Name anything. What do you wish for?" Bob said, "I just want my buddies back …"

I'll never forget the time I was chasing my little sister around. I was probably eleven years old, and Shelly was nine. As we were running around in circles behind a fast-food place, she slipped. She bumped her head on the wall. I noticed that she didn't cry at all. But suddenly, when she looked over at the wall, she saw a big red splotch on the surface of that wall. She started screaming out in pain. In her mind, she was seeing blood, and she thought her head was cracked open.

I walked over and showed her that the red color was actually red paint. It wasn't blood. She stopped crying. We both started laughing. Well, at least I did. What changed? Nothing. And everything. The difference was the way she was looking at the wall. When her perspective was painful, she was in agony. When she reframed her point-of-view, she felt okay again. Sure, I probably got a tongue-lashing the second we got home, but my point remains.

Chances are you "locked-in" to your particular sense of self when you were a little boy or girl. Something happened to you, or in you, and you latched on to it. In your little heart of hearts you said, "Well that's me." *I'm the dumb one. I'm the girl nobody sees. I'm the unlucky guy.* Well, I'm here to tell you that *that story is not you.* It's just a story, an interpretation. You are you. And everything can change when you change your point-of-view.

When she was five-years-old, my daughter Katie said she *really* believed in Peter Pan. She meant business She wrote him a letter. "I love you, Peter Pan. I want to be your best friend. Signed, Katie." Guess what? He wrote back! Several adults conspired to make this happen, of course, but it all started with her premise: *Peter Pan is real, and I'm going to connect with him.* And she got a letter back in the mail from Peter Pan. She still has it. And she *still* believes. Unfortunately, she's in junior high school now, so it's sort of a mixed blessing. I kid. I kid.

Psychologists in Pennsylvania discovered something incredible. They found a way to convince people that a rubber hand was actually their own. The rubber hand was set up on a table in front of participants, alongside their real hand. But their real hand was hidden from sight behind a little partition. Since the hand they could see was the rubber hand, that was the hand they ended up believing was real. After simultaneously touching the real hand and the fake hand, researchers would thwack the rubber hand with a hammer—and the people would recoil and flinch as if their real hand had been hit. The now-famous "rubber-hand illusion" is not only a mind-blowing party trick, it shows us two things:

1) Psychologists in Pennsylvania have way too much

time on their hands, rubber or otherwise.

2) We base our sense of reality on what we perceive, not based on "facts."

Michael Jordan is the greatest basketball player in history. We can see that now. But he saw it first. MJ has said, "You have to *expect* things of yourself before you can do them." Which "self" is running your life? *You must decide.* According to the Founder of Strategic Coach, Dan Sullivan, you actually have several selves:

Your "Past-Based Self." If you live from this self, you will be resistant to change. You will be fixated on your past. You will feel that what is most meaningful in your life has *already* happened. If you define yourself this way, here's what you are going to experience: *Repetition and frustration.*

Your "Future-Based Self." If you operate your life from this future self (the person you imagine and yearn to become), you will create a very positive image of yourself. You will be attracted to new ideas, and you will welcome bigger challenges. You don't reject the past. You build on it, learn from it, and grow into the person you long to be.

Either your past- or future-based self-concept will take control of the steering wheel of your life. It's like the story of the two dogs:

A Native American chief told his son a story. "Inside of you there are two dogs," the chief said. "One of the dogs will bite you and bark at you—he wants to destroy you. The other dog will protect and support you—he will guide you into beautiful fields. Son, the bad dog fights the good dog all of the time." The boy asked his dad, "Which dog wins?" The wise father reflected for a moment and replied, "The one you feed the most."

Don't be like the guy who owned a dangerous pit bull. He loved the animal because every time the dog would tear his arm off, he would bring it back to him.

Don't feed the dog that is bent on destroying you. Don't let other people define you. Don't let others tell you how to look at your life. Rock legend Frank Zappa sure didn't. Joe Pine was a reporter who had a wooden leg. When he interviewed Zappa, Pine said, "With your long hair, from where I am sitting you could be a woman." Frank Zappa replied, "From where I am sitting you could be a table."

AHA! Lesson #2

Get a new lens on life.

Questions to ask yourself when it's pouring rain outside *or* the remote is broken:

- What six-word story describes your life as you look back on it? Yeah, six words. Here are some examples.

All but the last two are from a wonderful book called *Six-Word Memoirs.*

Son of architect, had no structure.
—Whitney Cox

Found true love, married someone else.
—Bjorn Stromberg

Afraid of everything. Did it anyway.
—Ayse Erginer

Atheist alcoholic gets sober through God.
—Bob Todd

Never really finished anything except cake.
—Carletta Perkins

Fell in love. Married. Divorced. Repeat.
—Lori McLeese

Became my mother. Please shoot me.
—Cynthia Kaplan

I am the one who knocks.
—Walter White

Retirement is not in my vocabulary.
—Betty White

Six words can reveal so much about you and the way you perceive your life. Try this. Write six words that describe your life as you look back on it. Then write six words that describe the life you want for your future. For example ...

I keep driving around in circles.
—Tom Johnson **(past)**

Found my map! Now on track.
—Tom Johnson **(future)**

For goodness sake, ask for directions!
—Tom Johnson's wife

- What six-word story describes the life you want looking forward?
- What results do you keep getting in your life?
- How are those patterns connected to the way you see things?
- What point of view has you "hooked?"
- How do you want to see yourself and your future?

3

YOUR ACTIONS ARE A JOKE

I just wish my mouth had a backspace key.
—Alan Connor

A hot young comedian was feeling cocky. He was all set to impress the old timers at the weekly gathering of professional comics in New York City. These veterans of show business had been meeting for years. They were so familiar with a collection of a hundred classic jokes they would simply say the joke *number*, and the group would bust up with laughter.

The new comic had studied the jokes, but that didn't make the event any less amazing. He sat and watched in awe. Morty yelled out, "Number six!" The whole group cracked up. "Hey, number 28," said another old pro. Lots of laughter and applause followed. This went on for about an hour. Finally the young comedian felt confident enough to jump in. He chose a joke he knew was a crowd-pleaser. He shouted out, "Hey guys … number 17!" He got nothing. Zip. No response. You could have heard a pin drop. A few awkward moments later another of the experienced comics blurted out, "Number 88." And the whole room broke into sidesplitting laughter.

After the meeting the young stand-up approached one of the old-time veterans. "Hey, how come nobody laughed at *my* joke? Number 17 is a great one." The old guy leaned in. "Yeah, that is a really good one, Kid. But you gotta work on your delivery."

It's not just the joke, it's the telling that makes it wonderful or terrible. The same is true in your life. It's not enough to have the right formula for living or happiness. To become who you were meant to be means you have to *deliver* on the promise of you. We have looked at how your set-up creates meaning in your life, and how the way you look at things changes things. So, what should you do when you find the right set-up for your life? You *act like you mean it*. You adopt the habits of the person you want to become.

It takes practice to become a great joke teller and to create a strong act. You need to know what to say, how to say it, what words to punch up, and when to pause to build up the suspense … just before the big payoff. You must master your "act." Malcolm Gladwell unpacked this idea in his book *Outliers* when he showed how the top athletes, musicians, and artists all spent approximately 10,000 hours getting great at doing what they do. You've spent at least that many hours thinking about your life, and those are hours of practice you may have to now override.

You won't experience meaningful growth in your life until you take massive action in the direction of your best you. I'm not talking about intentions. I know dozens of funny people, but they haven't put in the time to turn pro. I'm talking about ACTION.

Have you noticed that you judge yourself based on your intentions while you judge others based on their actions? George Carlin said that everyone who goes faster than you on the highway is an idiot and anyone going slower is a moron. Sound familiar?

> *Socrates was a famous Greek teacher who went around giving people advice. They killed him.*
> —Junior high school history student

Two ways to know precisely what's important to you

Take a look at your own actions. It's not always pleasant.

Do it anyway. You can talk about your values, your family, your favorite charities. But it's easy to discover what your priorities are. Take a look at two things: 1. Your watch. 2. Your wallet. (Hey, if you are under thirty, and you don't look at a watch to tell time, you can look at your phone to follow along here.) I want you to look at your daily habits. *How do you spend your time and money?*

Like the woman who came home from the grocery store and told her husband, "Honey, start packing your suitcase because I won the lottery." Her husband says, "That's great … a vacation! Should I pack for warm weather or cold?" His wife says, "That's up to you, 'cause I'm rich, and you're out of here."

The way you spend your time and your money says it all. Notice that the word "spend" describes both. You spend your time. You spend your money. Again, it's what you invest your life in that defines you. You might say you love your kids, but love is a four-letter word spelled T-I-M-E. And don't tell me you believe in social causes if you don't put your money where your morality is.

There is a classic principle in self-help literature called the "act-as-if" principle. Lots of motivational techniques don't really work, but this one does. It's been described in different ways. "What would you *do* if you knew you could not fail?" "Act as is *if* you had the thing you most wanted." "Dress the part." "Be the ball." You catch the drift. Act. As. If. (Warning: Be smart about how you do this.

In first grade I went to school with a Superman outfit on under my clothes. I thought I'd fly home for recess. Instead the cape fell down and got caught when I flushed the toilet, and I nearly choked to death.)

Fake it 'till you make it?

In my field, the "act-as-if" principle is called Show *Business*. You put on a show. Professional comedians and entertainers call their stage performance the same thing: their "act." This doesn't mean they are faking it or pretending. It means they get up there and do it. And they do it night after night. And finally they get good at it. And their "act" becomes great. That's the difference between an amateur and a professional comedian. An amateur will continually tweak his "new routine" for the same old audience. A professional will perform the same ACT for a brand new audience. Act like a pro.

Harry Houdini's great rival Howard Thurston was perhaps the greatest magician of the twentieth century. One day a kid walked up to him and said, "Mr. Thurston, I can do 50 different amazing magic tricks." The master magician responded by saying, "How interesting; I do eight." *What have you mastered?*

"To be is to do"
—Socrates

"To do is to be"
—Sartre

"Do be do be do"
—Sinatra

You're not just a human being or a human seeing. *You're a human doing.* Think about it. When a spiritual guru urges you to find solitude and peace, he advises you to "just be." But notice that the wise teacher then immediately tells you specifically what to DO in order to just be. "Practice yoga." "Pray." "Meditate for 30 minutes." And so, "Just be with nature" turns into something active like, "Take a walk in the woods."

Don't forget that you don't just have a body. You are a body. Your body is wired for doing—walking, talking, running, breathing, eating, dancing, laughing, sleeping, hugging. Life is a nonstop series of doing something. The good news is this: *You can act on purpose.* And when you do, your life will feel more meaningful. You have to keep at it. Don't be like the Kamikaze Flight School Instructor who told his students: "Watch closely. I'm only going to do this once."

Ever hear the story of the three frogs that were sitting on a branch? One of the frogs decided to jump off. How many were left? Three. The one frog only *decided* to jump. Once you decide, you have to actually jump. Your emotions will follow your motions. Have you been stuck for a long time waiting to feel a certain way before you believe you can take action? Well, as Gene Wilder (Willy Wonka) once said, "Strike that. Reverse it." Take action and the feelings will follow. Act. As. If.

I do this experiment at the end of my keynote speech. I have the entire audience stand up. I say, "Okay, everybody put a big smile on your face—even if it's a fake I'm-at-work phony type of smile. Do it. Now, while you are smiling, I want you to raise your hands up high toward the ceiling and look up. Hey, suddenly you are all Pentecostal people." Everybody does what I say—probably because I have the microphone. Then, when these 300 or so people are all standing up, looking up, and raising their hands up, I ask them to sincerely try to feel down. They can't do it. It's hard to feel down when you are physically looking up. Remember that kids' song? *"If you're happy and you know it, look up, wave your hands and act like an idiot!"* Well, however it went, it made you feel good.

Behave your way into the feelings you want

Have you ever noticed that when you get invited to a party you don't want to go to, you dread the thought of going for days? But ... when the day arrives, you show up anyway. You grumble at first. But you put on the outfit. You get there and start giving out handshakes and hugs. You eat some chips and dip. And pretty soon, you notice something. You're actually having a wonderful time. Why? You have been *acting* like you want to be there. And by acting the way you want to feel, you start feeling the way you want to feel. Imagine if instead of letting this happen when it happens, you did it on purpose? Act. As. If. Do this on purpose.

My friend Mark Matteson is a motivational speaker who knows how to spark people to success. It's all about taking action. Mark says, "Unassertive salespeople have skinny kids." Frank Bettger wrote what many consider to be the greatest book ever written on salesmanship. It's called *How I Raised Myself From Failure to Success Through Selling.* Bettger was a professional baseball player. He was on the verge of getting cut from his team. He made one change that made him a crowd favorite, quadrupled his income, and led to him becoming a super successful insurance agent after his baseball career had ended. He took steroids. No, wait, that's today's baseball players. Frank *ACTED like he was wildly enthusiastic about what he was doing.*

If you are married, imagine if you had acted toward your spouse during the dating phase of your relationship, like you act now. Would he/she have stuck with you? Yikes. Probably not. You wowed your partner with your enthusiasm for him or her. You paid attention. You said, "I love you." And you acted like you meant it. Gifts. Gestures. Acts of service. Physical affection. It put you both into a state of bliss. In fact, the more you acted like you were in love, the more you fell in love.

A number of years ago I attended a powerful seminar called *Money & You.* Rather than a mind-numbing series of lectures, this workshop had participants taking action and learning from live games that related to our relationship with money. Julie was our instructor. She said, "Okay, you are each going to get some toy rings. I want you to toss them onto these sticks. If you go to the back of the room you can take a long shot and win $100 if you get your ring onto the stick. If you want to take a close shot, just three feet away, you win, but you only get $1."

Something interesting happened. I made a realization. Like everybody else, I wanted to take the long shot. To hit the 3-pointer so to speak, to smack in the home run, to win the $100 bill. So I headed to the back of the room. I took one of the toy rings and chucked it up into the air. I missed the stick by about twenty feet. In fact, my ring hit the ceiling and bounced off some bald guy's head.

I thought about this scenario and had a mini-epiphany. "If I take the really close shot I can score every time." It dawned on me that I could repeat that effective action over and over again. So I did. I successfully made the first toss, the second, the third, and so on. It took me about ten minutes but I racked up about $200 in play money before anybody else even hit the long shot to win the $100. The lesson for me: Take the right action. Get great at it. Repeat. It starts with working on the right thing—the thing that's you. Frank Sinatra didn't move pianos.

Put this into practice in your love life. Stop trying to make big "fix it" romantic gestures in favor of doing lots of little acts of love. (It's fun trying to convince your spouse that ten meals at Wendy's far surpass one meal at Ruth's Chris Steak House.)

Get your act together

You can tell in the first few seconds when a comedian walks on stage whether you are going to enjoy his performance. It's a gut reaction thing. It comes down to this: does he look and act confident? If the answer is yes, you sit back and happily go along for the ride. But have you ever heard an unprepared speaker walk up to the podium and say something like, "I didn't really have time to plan what I was going to say this morning, but here goes." You want to find the exit immediately. You think to yourself, "Why is he even up there if he doesn't have something valuable to tell me?" The best speakers and entertainers mean business. And they act like it.

One of my worst on-stage experiences happened when I was twenty-two years old. I had just made the move to "full-time working pro." Back when I was seventeen, I became a junior member of the world-famous

Magic Castle in Hollywood. I auditioned while in high school and they said, "Your magic is not that great … but you are really funny, so we're going to let you in." Flash forward five years. I had a chance to perform in the big room, the Palace of Mystery. My performance would be an audition, to see if I was ready for the big leagues. But instead of doing my regular act, which was honed and worked like a charm, I decided I wanted to wow the Magic Castle magicians with all new material. What a mistake. I got stuck standing in front of a live audience worrying about every movement I made. I tried out all new magic tricks and new—i.e., untested—jokes. I bombed. I couldn't even see the audience clearly. The sweat from my forehead was running right into my eyes. I was bombing while my eyes were burning. I didn't land that gig. But I learned a key lesson as a performer: when trying out new material, wear a headband. Also, focus on your main routine and turn it into a well-honed ACT.

Keep failing … forward

Flash forward two more years. I was booked to perform at a magic convention in Iowa. After several flights and a grueling travel schedule, I got to my hotel room. I was wiped out and decided to take a short nap before my performance. Well, I didn't wake up. I slept through the alarm. I woke up right at the time I was supposed to start my performance when I heard a pounding on my door. "You are on in three minutes, Adam!" I got up in a daze. I threw my clothes on. I ran to the ballroom and took 60 seconds to set up my props. I was still half-asleep when I did my act in front of a live audience. I wasn't even awake enough to feel nervous. But I wowed that crowd. Why? I stuck with the act that I had performed hundreds of times before. It's true. There's something to that old saying, "I could do that in my sleep."

I've seen many wannabe entertainers fall into a trap. I call it the "lightning-will-strike" trap. These fledgling comedians go looking for the perfect new joke that they hope will suddenly make them famous. If they're magicians, they go looking for the next cool new trick that will make them a star. These guys go to magic conventions, they buy the new floating rose trick. Or maybe they learn some amazing finger-flinging, sleight-of-hand moves they practice in front of the bathroom mirror. But then they go back to their day jobs selling furniture at Sears, because nobody cares about the flashy new joke or trick. They never polished their ACT. You have to get your ACT together if you want to make it in the big leagues. WARNING: Don't work on your weaknesses. If you do, you'll just have stronger weaknesses. Find what you are great at and work on it. Polish it. Get your act together.

AHA! Lesson #3

ACT like you mean it.

Questions to ask yourself while hearing "your call is important to us" when on hold:

- What should you be doing to become who you were meant to be?
- What are you doing instead of what you should be doing?
- How should you be acting?
- What does that look like?
- Where does it happen?
- When does it happen?
- How will you spend your time and money so that you can act on purpose?

4

YOUR FEARS ARE A JOKE

When I told people I wanted to be a comedian, they laughed. They're not laughing now.

—Bob Monkhouse

I get nervous *every* time I walk up to the stage. In fact, if I don't, then I get nervous about why I'm not nervous.

It's been that way since I was a kid. Even as the class clown, I'd get that rush of fear just before I would make a wise crack in front of Mrs. Whipple's fifth grade class. I'd say, "What do you call a dog with no front legs?" Pause. Wait for what seems like forever when it's really just a second. Wait for the silence to draw the class right into the punch line. And then say it, "… Scooter!"

"What do you call a dog with no legs at all?" Pause again. "It doesn't matter, he won't come when you call him!"

Boom. They laughed (This was back in the days when pets were not considered fully human family members). But I have felt that oh-no-I'm-about-to-look-stupid kind of fear every time I have entertained, whether for pay … or for play. As I write this, I am in a hotel room prepping to host an international sales convention at an incredible resort in Laguna Beach, California. Yes, it's awesome. Sometimes I take these gigs just to stock up on the tiny shampoos. The weather and the view are spectacular. But I am having a hard time enjoying it because I'm worried about the 27-page awards script I have to read in a few hours in front of 300 people. Will I mess up the pronunciation of Xiao De Liu as he comes up to receive his coveted award? Will my tuxedo look cool or will it look like something I rented for the junior prom back in the 1980s?

People are more afraid of speaking in public than they are of death. That's because, when you pass away, they cover you up. But when you die on stage, you still have to stand there. Comedians choose words like "killing," "slaying," and "destroying" for when they actually please an audience. I have talked to performers after a gig and asked, "Hey Mike, how did you do with that Health & Human Services group?" I hear,

"I MASSACRED them!" And my answer is, "Wow, that's great ... sounds like they *loved* you."

What entertainers (and soldiers) know is this: you have to put yourself on the line and work with/through/beyond/in/around/over/past your fears to get to the good stuff. *You have to go through what you fear to get what you want.* If you want anything—a relationship, a baby, a business, a new start—you must do the thing you fear. You can't erase it 'til you face it.

The biggest "break" I ever got as a young performer was from a group that virtually no one has heard of. It was called WOW. They were the Wondrous Order of Wizards. A dear old magician named Mr. Zweers—he was actually in his 50s but he cultivated the old mentor role to great effect—worked with a group of teenagers from 14 to 18 years old. It was sort of an underground club for aspiring magicians. We met in a secret basement of a bank on Sunset and Vine in Hollywood. You had to ring a bell to be allowed through a door that led to an elevator that led to a splendid little theater, a museum with Houdini's actual hand cuffs, and most important of all, a chance to perform in front of live audiences. *That's* the most important thing for a performer: Conquering your stage fright by "doing time" on stage.

You had to audition to become a member of the Wondrous Order of Wizards. Though I was frightened sick,

I signed for an audition slot. I stood on that stage to do my magic act. It didn't go well at first. My hand was *shaking* as I tried to load the jumbo playing card into the secret compartment so it could disappear. When I finally made it vanish and wrapped up my show, they applauded me. But then the moment of truth came. Mr. Zweers sent me to the "Green Room" so that the WOW members could vote on whether I would be accepted into this magical society. I didn't even know what a "Green Room" was. I looked for green paint color on the walls. When I found the right room, I sat there for what felt like three hours. It was probably 10 minutes.

One of the WOW members, Jon Levy—who a few years later would introduce me to David Copperfield—came into the room to give me the verdict. He was as serious as a heart attack. He sat down across from me and let me have it. "This is a really special and private group. We liked your act. We liked it a lot. But I'm sorry to tell you that we just don't think you're a good fit for our group."

I was devastated.

He walked me back to the theater where Mr. Zweers and ten or so young magicians were waiting. I was holding back tears as I walked into that little auditorium.

They burst into wild applause. They started laughing uproariously. This was their "initiation" process. I had gone through it. I felt that fear and auditioned anyway.

I had made it. I was accepted. My whole future as a professional entertainer was on the other side of that fear.

What you want is on the other side of fear

Life is like that. You have to pass through the fear to experience the fun. Being in that group, to use the #1 most worn-out phrase of the last 50 years, *changed my life*. It really did. As Susan Jeffers once said, "Feel the fear and do it anyway." If I had felt the fear and not done it, I would have been robbed of one of my greatest experiences (and probably my career), right at the beginning of high school.

Speaking of magic and secrets … I have learned something important about fear. Have you noticed that how you feel about what you think can cripple you? Here is a secret weapon for breaking through when the emotion of fear has you held hostage. You must *change the way you think about what you feel.* When I am about to get up to entertain, for example, I still feel the nerves—but instead of worrying about it, I smile with anticipation. Here's why: Fear is connected to an emotional-physical reaction that courses through your body like 150 ounces of espresso. It's called adrenalin. It can be a powerful thing.

Remember those stories of 80-year-old women

lifting up pick-up trucks to save a grandkid trapped underneath? (When I hear those stories I always wonder why the woman let her grandkids play under the truck in the first place.) In situations like that, there's no time for steroids. A rush of adrenalin floods your system and strengthens you. Fear, when you think of it this way, empowers you. This comes back to one of our big themes: *Things don't happen to you, they happen for you.* If you want to make a splash, you've got to climb those steps up to the high diving board. There will be a moment of dread, of terror, of panic. But you have to jump. "Cannonball!" Comedians have to do it every night. Why not you?

More good news: According to the Bloomfield Commission on Human Fear and Transformation, 99.3% of the things you fear will happen, never happen. Just think about when the following things have happened to you:

You saw a phone number on your cell phone, and you were afraid to pick up or listen to the voice mail message, for fear of it being terrible news. Turns out it was a misdial … or someone calling just to say "Hello!"

You dreaded eating vegetables as a kid. Even the *idea* of eating spinach made you nauseous. But when you tasted it again as an adult, it somehow magically transformed into an edible dish.

You got called into the principal's office (or your boss's

office) fearing the worst. And you were commended instead of reprimanded. Remember my story about running for 8th grade class president? When I was called into the Vice Principal's office I thought I was in trouble for gambling in the restroom with the guys. But when the vice principal sat me down, he said, "How'd you like to run for *school* president?"

As the eminent philosopher and reality show celebrity Gary Busey likes to say, "Fear is an acronym that stands for False. Expectations. Appearing. Real." Oh, I almost forgot. The "Bloomfield Commission on Human Fear and Transformation?" I made up that fictional organization to *frame* how you would look at what I was going to say next. Hey, it's my book. I can do that kind of thing to make a point. *Don't allow made-up fears frame your life experiences.*

The children's story of Jumbo, the circus elephant with giant ears, illustrates this idea perfectly. After one show Jumbo noticed a tiny mouse in the circus tent. The mouse kept following him around. Jumbo became terribly frightened and ran out of the tent. He ran as fast as he could. But the mouse followed and was right on his tail. Jumbo ran and ran. But the little mouse kept gaining on him. Finally, out of breath and dangerously close to the railroad tracks, Jumbo stopped. Facing his fear, he turned around and with a terrified voice asked the mouse, "What is it you want from me?"

The tiny mouse, huffing and puffing after the long chase said, "Please Sir. May I please have your autograph?"

What you don't know can hurt you ... if you let it

As a father, husband, entertainer, entrepreneur, filmmaker, magician, comedian, motivational speaker, youth pastor, salesman, personal coach, and earthquake survivor, I have felt fear many times, but I don't think I was ever more afraid than I was one particular night. It was Valentine's Day. I was 17 years old. I came home that night with no date and no girlfriend. Normally my parents and sister were home. That night nobody was there.

What was even more strange, was that ALL of the lights outside of the house were OFF. As I walked into the house I felt an eerie feeling about that. *Why are all of the lights out?*

I opened the door and went into the house and my fear increased immediately. There were no lights on anywhere inside the place. My mom never left the house like this—it was completely dark. I felt alone. Afraid.

Well, I needed to go to the bathroom. But before I went in, I walked around the house and turned on every light I could think of. I flipped on the light in the hall, in the family room, my bedroom, the living room.

Ah. I felt safer. So I went into the bathroom. Closed the door. I turned that light on too, and did my business. Then, when I opened the door I noticed that *all the lights in the house were off again.*

I stood there completely frozen. I was petrified. I didn't

know what to do. I figured, *if I run outside they'll grab me. If I just stand here, they'll attack me.* I pictured Chucky, Jason, Freddy Krueger, all the worst horror creeps. I was sure my life was about to end. I darted into my bedroom. My heart was pounding with fear. I locked the door by sliding my baseball bat between my dresser and my door.

I stood there in a frozen hypnotic daze. I thought to myself, *They know I'm here. I'm a sitting duck here in my bedroom. I don't want to die. I've got to make a run for it.* I ran out of the house. I was running faster than a contestant runs up to the stage of the *Price is Right* when their name is called.

I jumped into my car. It wouldn't start. It was all so horrifying. I heard a helicopter flying overhead. I may have used up an entire lifetime supply of adrenaline that night.

But in the end, it was all for nothing.

Nothing horrific or criminal had actually occurred that night. Nothing usually does. After I got my car started, I went to a friend's house. His dad went back to the house with me. We had flashlights and baseball bats. We saw somebody in the window.

It turned out to be my younger sister, Shelly.

She had been in the house the whole time. She went through every room in our house and turned *off* all of the lights when she saw me drive up. After I turned them all *on* and went into the bathroom, she came out of her room and turned every single light back off—and just waited to see how I would react.

Later she told me that I stood there like a piece of petrified wood when I opened the door and saw that everything was pitch black. She thought it was hilarious. I thought it was going to be the end of my life. I had imagined the worst. But 99.99 percent of what you fear will never happen, and that night, none of it happened. Your mind can play worse tricks on you than even your sister. Take it from this magician. Fear is not a fun illusion.

In your life you *will* experience fear. It's a given. If you don't deal with your fears, they will deal with you. And cripple you. And paralyze you. Your weapon for overcoming fear is simple: Face it. Take action. Whatever you most want is on the other side of fear.

AHA! Lesson #4

Put feared things first.

Questions to ask yourself next time your mind takes you on a terrifying trip:

- When were you most afraid? Was your fear well-founded? How did you get through it?

- What is the most courageous thing you have ever done? What fear did you have to overcome to do it?
- What courageous thing do you need to do next in your life?
- How will your life change if you do it?
- What is the specific fear you must face in order to accomplish your biggest dream?
- What action can you take immediately to face and erase your fear?
- Will you do it? What steps do you need to take to start?

5

YOUR GOALS ARE A JOKE

Hot dog vendor: "Hey pal, what can I make ya?"
Buddhist Monk: "Make me ONE WITH EVERYTHING."
—Anonymous

As soon as those sponge bunnies magically appeared in my hand at age nine, I KNEW I wanted to be a magician and a comedian when I grew up. I made cassette tape recordings that I would play back for myself: "You can do it. You can become a professional magician." I was thrilled when my friend Chris's mom printed my first business card. I was thirteen years old (and had a different name than I do now—but that's a story for another chapter.) The day the box of cards arrived, I felt like I was really in show business.

The business cards read:

MARK BROWN, MAGICIAN
"Magic for All Occasions"

On the bottom of the card was a black top hat. And of course my phone number. When your unique selling proposition is "Magic for ALL Occasions," it means one thing for sure: you'll mostly be doing birthday parties. My first paying gig was at a Shakey's Pizza restaurant. It was a little girl's birthday bash. Her dad gave me $5 and all the pizza I could eat. Not sure if they liked the show, but I certainly made a lot of pizza disappear that day. I was in heaven.

I started working quite a bit as a performer, but I was not yet a good marketer. One day I got a phone call from a man who said, "Hi. My name is Tony, and I have fifty dollars to spend on a magic show for my son's birthday party." I responded back instantly. "Hi Tony, I only charge forty!" What a master negotiator. I was haggling against myself. Turned out it was Tony Perkins of the movie *Psycho* fame. I did a show in the Hollywood Hills for his son Elvis and a few weeks later for his other son, Osgood. I'm *not* making these names up. Google them and see. When I magically made a real live bunny rabbit appear, one of the rich kids said, "Who gets him?"

The gigs kept coming, but I wondered if I should get a "real job." That was what most people seemed to think was the correct path, so I got a "real job." I worked as a custodian in college—for one day—and in that one day I had a "personal punch line" moment, a sudden revelation. "Hey, I could make more money in thirty minutes doing my magic show, and it would not involve cleaning up after a boss who can't hit the potty target." I quit and focused on my magic. Soon enough I graduated from college, got married, and went full-time as an entertainer. My new business card wasn't much better than the first one. It read:

ADAM CHRISTING, COMEDIAN & MAGICIAN
"Entertainment from Another Dimension"

This was weird, vague, and terrible all at once. What did *"Entertainment from Another Dimension"* mean exactly? It sounded like season one of *The Twilight Zone*. But I started working a lot. I was newly married. My wife was student teaching. We had no money. We were living off the money we got returning wedding gifts. I started making fifty cold calls a day to get gigs. It was tough— not only the cold calling, which is always tough, but the groping for what it was I was really offering people when I was offering "entertainment from another dimension." I got enough gigs to stay afloat—barely.

Then one day, my friend Cary Trivanovich (a mime) invited me to breakfast. I told Cary about my cold-calling efforts, and shared with him my vague wish for something more solid and more in line with my beliefs about life and entertainment. I knew I was different from other comedians, I just didn't know how I was different, or how I could use that difference to my advantage. I kept asking myself what "the other dimension" was, and I kept not being able to answer. As I floundered around trying to define it, or describe it—*it's getting big laughs without getting raunchy or racial*—Cary heard something. Not longer after that, he gave me the idea for *Clean Comedians*.

And just like a joke that floors you, I felt a sudden shift in my life. THIS IS IT! I knew I had been given what I would later find out is called a brand. I knew exactly what I wanted. I wanted to create an entertainment business called *Clean Comedians*—a company that integrated my professional aspirations and my personal beliefs. The *other dimension* turned out to be simply, clean. It was a profound realization—right under my nose. The very next day I drove downtown to Los Angeles City Hall and got a business license. I was now Adam Christing, "Doing Business As" *Clean Comedians*.

The secret of living is to find the pivot of a concept on which you can make your stand.
—Luigi Pirandello

It doesn't have to be filthy to be funny!

It was 1990. In the early '90s comedy clubs were cleaning up. But stand-up comics were getting dirty. Even the joke set-ups were vulgar. My friend Steve Bridges and I would get big laughs making fun of the dirty guys. Like doing an impression of Andrew Dice Clay working clean: "Good evening this is Dice ... Good night." The *Clean Comedians* concept allowed me to re-frame funny for thousands of people who wanted to be entertained without feeling embarrassed.

Back then I knew almost nothing about running a business, but despite my ignorance, *Clean Comedians* grew and grew. It was clearly beneficial to event planners who couldn't afford to offend their clients or their bosses. They were thrilled to have a company they could trust. We started getting bookings from schools, churches, corporations, colleges, and even casinos. When I was invited to be a guest on a 50,000-watt radio station, I knew we needed a motto. I tinkered around with, "No blue for you," then, "Fun is not a four-letter word," but eventually I settled on: "It doesn't have to be filthy to be funny!"

As a young entrepreneur, I made every mistake in the book, and dozens that were not even in the book. One day, I had over 100 advertising flyers printed. We mailed them to theaters, associations, and businesses. But there was a typo I didn't catch before they went out. Instead of mentioning our motto, "It doesn't have to be filthy to be funny!" It said this, "*Clean Comedians* is an association of professional comedians who believe that: 'It doesn't have to be funny!'

It was a wild ride. By 2004, the company had booked nearly 200 different speakers, comedians, magicians, variety acts, impressionists, celebrities, and more. The gigs were coming in from everywhere. And though I was booking dozens of other performers, I was still performing at many of the events myself. In August 1992, I did 62 separate performances. One night I would do a show at Caesars Palace in Lake Tahoe. The next morning I would be at a junior high school in Riverside, California. It was exhilarating, and my wife and I were no longer selling crystal pitchers to pay the rent, but it was an unsustainable pace.

It takes a dream to make a dream come true

In December of 2004, I had written down over twenty things I wanted to accomplish in 2005. This was a habit I'd implemented each New Year that I thought was pretty great, but this approach to accomplishment was soon to be smashed by an encounter I had with Richard "Mack" Machowicz, a former Navy Seal. (Mack went on to host the TV show *Deadliest Warrior*). This guy is a trip. He has studied deeply in Zen Buddhism. He's also a trained military machine. Basically, he's a guy who can quickly kill you with his hands, and then pray a beautiful blessing over your dead body. After reading his powerful book, *Unleash The Warrior Within*, I called him and asked if I could hire him for a few hours of private coaching. (It's been exciting to discover that most authors will communicate with you personally if you reach out to them.)

He said he would come to my office. When Mack arrived that morning, he kind of freaked out our receptionist … but in a good way. He carried himself with ease and authority. When she told him that I was on a phone call, he waited outside my office in an almost meditative trance. But as soon as he walked in my door, it was game-on. I excitedly showed Mack my many goals for the New Year. I was proud to show him how many goals I was aiming to reach. He asked me to describe each one briefly. When I was done, he said, "Great, now we are going to eliminate nearly all of them … " What?

All my life, I've always wanted to be somebody,
but I see now I should have been more specific.
—Lily Tomlin

He said, "Adam, walk over to your light switch there on the wall and turn the light off." It felt like I was back in kindergarten. But I did it. He said, "Well done. Now, please walk over and turn the light back on." I did. Mack said, "Notice what you did? You took a straight line to accomplish one thing.

Notice that you didn't get up, make some coffee, phone a friend, search the web, get something to eat, and then turn off the light switch? You went right to it and accomplished the mission." That simple but profound exercise was the essence of Mack's message to me that day. But he hit me hard with it. Repeatedly.

"Adam, what ONE thing could you do that would create a breakthrough for you? What ONE thing do you want to achieve that will create the biggest win for you?" I saw it immediately: I said, "If I sell my *Clean Comedians* business I will have the freedom to pursue these other dream goals." Mack said, "Great. Then THAT is your *one* goal for 2005. You can work on the other ones after you sell the business." He made it crystal clear. *If you know what you want, you can have it.*

I got it. Identify your goal. Pursue it directly. But I thought maybe I needed more coaching from Mack that day. I was already planning to pay him $1,000 for his visit. I said, "Hey, can we walk down to the coffee shop, and I can pick your brain some more?" He said, "Sure, if that will help you." When we got to the restaurant I said, "There's more to it, right?" Mack said, "Not really." I said, "Hold on, if I could only get one huge secret from you, a formula for great Navy Seal-like accomplishment, what would you tell me?" He leaned in and said. "Adam. Hit. The. %$#*#. TARGET!" Then, very politely he said, "Are we done here?" And, with incredible charisma, he invited me to pay him an extra

$500. And I still had to pick up the check for the coffee. But there's a lesson in that: You are far more likely to "get" what you pay for.

Best money I ever spent. My original looooong list of goals for the upcoming year included things like: write and direct a "mockumentary" movie, build a new web business, produce a historical documentary film, and many other outlandish things. As I look back on that list today, I'm shocked that I ended up accomplishing most of the big things on that list. But it all happened because I focused on ONE critical target at a time. And the first was to sell my business. I geared everything my team did around that goal. I incentivized my staff with big bonuses to help sell the business. I hired a publicist to make the company more visible. We broke our sales record. I hired a business broker to sell it. Seven months later it was SOLD. Seven years later I wanted *Clean Comedians* back, and recently was able to make that happen too. *If you know what you want and lock-in on your target, you can have it.*

What do you want?

We walk around whining because we feel like we never get what we want. The truth is pretty much the opposite. You nearly always get what you want when, 1) You know what you want; and, 2) You want it real bad. Sometimes I give a motivational talk to high school students. It's called "Say YES to your Dreams." I open the program with this quotation: "Only a storm of hot passion can turn the destinies of people. And he alone can arouse passion who bears it within himself." I then ask the students, "What famous leader spoke those words?"

All kinds of answers come from the audience. "Obama!" "Mother Teresa!" "Steve Jobs!" Usually some kid will laugh and say, "You did." But when I tell them the correct historical answer, a hush comes over the auditorium. "Adolph Hitler … "

Hitler wrote those words while he was in prison. They are in his book *Mein Kampf* ("My Struggle"). I tell the students, "Hitler knew exactly what he wanted to do, and he created a burning passion to accomplish it." Of course I tell them that if he could use the principle of *focused passion* for evil, we can certainly use it for good. You might be thinking, "Um, how did we go from humor to Hitler?" Well, please remember that besides being humor-less and evil, Hitler was, at his core, a performance artist. The power of intense passion is hard to exaggerate. And it can be used for good.

One of America's great heroes is Martin Luther King Jr. In King's most famous speech he said, "I have a dream that my four little children will one day live in a nation where they will not be judged by the color of their skin but by the content of their character." I want you to notice two things. First, he was very specific about what he wanted. He wanted something very particular for his four children's future. It wasn't something vague like, "I want them to be happy," or "I want them to be proud." He wanted a world where his children *were not judged by the color of their skin*. It doesn't get more specific than the skin color of four little children.

Second, Dr. King let us feel the fire of his passion. Check out his "I Have a Dream" speech on YouTube. It still has the power to shake the earth. He changed the world through his focused passion. So, what about us? Our wants are wishy-washy. "I want to lose weight." Yes, but how much weight and when? "I want to make more money." Okay, but how much money and for what? "I want to be happier." Fine, but what does that look like? The point is that we can't reach goals that are not defined.

Goal! Goal! Goal!

Notice how in the world of sports, there tends to be a goal, a hoop, an end zone—something that makes it clear: "You scored!" That's also what you need in the game of life: something specific to shoot for. I was never great at soccer. I played it for about four years as a kid. Parents like soccer because they don't have to buy gloves and bats and balls, just some oranges every few weeks for halftime snacks. I played for fun and without much focus. But my four years of playing AYSO soccer culminated in one moment of greatness.

My team was the Dolphins, and we were in the championship game. I was not the star, just a wing guy. That's not high-profile in soccer. It's sort of like being the wing in the bucket of fried chicken. Everybody wants the breast or the drumstick. Well, I was the wing. The athletic brothers Danny and Timmy were the stars of our team, but that day nobody was scoring. The big game was tied. Scoreless. The parents were on the sidelines cheering us on (and of course living vicariously through our amazing athletic feats). Still, neither team scored. Our coach came up with a little incentive program during the last few minutes of the game. During a time-out he offered $2 to anybody who scored a goal. I wasn't motivated by money. All $2 could buy you was a Slurpee and a comic book. But I wanted to feel like a star. It was like performing on the field. I wanted to score the big goal. I wanted to win the game for our team and be the hero.

I considered tying all the shoelaces of the players on the other team together, but they wouldn't stand still. Then, like when I beat Robert to the finish line in my second grade class, I saw exactly what I wanted, and I pictured it wholeheartedly. I imagined myself scoring the winning goal. It was like it happened before it happened.

We ran back out on the field. One of my teammates kicked the ball hard. It hit the goal post but ricocheted off of the top bar. The rest of this memory plays out in slow motion for me. I jumped up higher than ever and headed the ball right into the net. We won the game! Parents went bonkers. My teammates lifted me up and took me off the field like a hero.

I got the two bucks, sure, but more importantly, I got what I *really* wanted that day: I helped my team win the game. I hit the target.

AHA! Lesson #5

If you know what you want, you can have it.

Questions to ask yourself when you feel under or overwhelmed:

- What EXACTLY do you want?
- What, specifically, is your target?
- What things can you take OFF your wish list in order to achieve your goal?
- Where are you stuck?
- What do you need to do to get what you want?
- Will you do it? When?

6

YOUR PAIN IS A JOKE

I respect wisdom but I obey pain.
—Anonymous

During a very somber church service, the senior minister walked up to the pulpit and sang in a dirge-like voice: "I'm the senior pastor of this church, I make $3,000 a month, that's not enough money."

Then, as if to top him, the younger associate minister came up to the platform. He sounded like a depressed monk and sang, "I'm the assistant minister of this church, I only make $2,000 a month, that's not enough money."

Finally, the organist took his turn. He sang, "I'm the organist of this church, I make $5,000 a week … THERE'S NO BUSINESS LIKE SHOW BUSINESS!"

When you tell a joke like that one above, you need to punch up the final line—really belt it out, and use hand-motions like you're playing the piano. You don't just tell the joke, you *live* the joke. That's how you grab an audience. You can't wait to capture a crowd's eyes and ears. From the moment you hit the stage, you need to do one thing immediately. You must grab the audience's *attention.*

One of my favorite attention-grabbing openers was what comedian Brett Leake said on his first appearance on *The Tonight Show* with Jay Leno. Brett has muscular dystrophy. When he first came on stage you could see how the terrible disease has affected his body. Brett began with this joke: "Hi I'm Brett Leake. I have a form of muscular dystrophy. Unless you're Christian Science. Then … I'm a hypochondriac."

What I love about Brett's joke is how his punch line hits us with an instant realization. We nod and say to ourselves, *"That's right, disease is real. Pain is real."* Brett uses humor to handle his hardship. *He has reframed his pain.* You can, too.

> *The worst time to have a heart attack is during a game of Charades.*
> —Demetri Martin

Pain forces you to take a look at what's hurting. A good joke makes you look at things differently too, because it sets you up, gives you some pain—some kind of setback—then surprises you with the punch line. My dad is a wonderful joke teller. Here's one of his favorite jokes. It's a story about putting your pain into a new frame of reference.

A patient is in agony in the hospital. He has excruciating pain in his foot, and the doctor comes into the room looking at an X-ray and says, "Well, I've got good news and bad news. Which do you want first?" The patient says, "I'll take the bad news first, Doc." The doctor tells him, "You have gangrene in your foot and I'm going to have to amputate it." The man says, "That's terrible, Doctor! Please, please tell me, what's the good news?" The doctor says, "The guy in the next bed wants to buy your slippers."

You have to *listen* to your pain before you can see it in a new way. Listening your way through a tough situation usually beats trying to talk your way through it. My stand-up comic friend Michael Jr. had to follow Chris Rock at a comedy club one night. Rock had the audience roaring. Rock rocked the room. So Michael Jr. was in a complete panic—which is to say he was in pain. He had to quickly figure out a way to follow him on stage. How do you get an audience's attention after that roller coaster?

Michael did something smart. He brought the energy down. Instead of going loud, he went quiet. Michael walked up to the mike and waited … and waited. Anticipation built. He drew them in. After a long pause he said very calmly, "Oh … sometimes the jokes don't come for a while." They loved it. He made them listen to him so that they could see his comedy in a way completely different from Chris Rock's stand-up persona.

And you must listen. You have to hear what your hurts are saying. Only then can you reframe them.

In his refreshingly honest book *The Problem of Pain*, C.S. Lewis writes, "We can ignore even pleasure. But pain insists upon being attended to. God whispers to us in our pleasures, speaks in our conscience, but shouts in our pains: it is his megaphone to rouse a deaf world." Before you can re-frame it, you have to allow pain to have your undivided attention. When you are really hurting, your first reaction is: *How in the world can I get out of this RIGHT NOW?* But what's crucial for your life is not *how* you get out of the pain—but rather *what* you get out of it.

> *Expecting life to treat you well because you are a good person is like expecting an angry bull not to charge you because you are a vegetarian.*
> —Shari Barr

Have you noticed when people actually get to the place where they can accept their cancer, divorce, job loss, or illness, they often end up saying: "__________ was the best thing that ever happened to me." Why would they say *that*? It goes back to what Steve Martin once wrote: "It's pain that changes our lives." Pain gives you a new vantage point—if you let it. How can this work for you? There are three steps. Take your pain and:

CLAIM it.

Don't medicate it away. Don't deny it or try to defy it. Feel it. It's tempting to think of pain as something that hits you from the outside. But until you own it as yours—from the inside—you can't begin to see it in a new light.

REFRAME it.

This is the key. You have to move from thinking, *This happened TO me* to believing, *This has happened FOR me.* In his book, *Look at More*, Andy Stephanovich says, "You won't find new solutions if you keep looking at things in the same ways."

EXPLAIN it.

Start talking about your pain in a way that empowers you and others. You are the hero (not the victim) of this story. Don't skip this step. *You live inside of the stories you tell yourself and repeat to others.* Be like the little boy who was digging in a heap of manure. When his friend asked him why, the little boy said, "I know there must be a pony under all of this!"

Let's be real. We don't *want* to change our opinions or perspective. We start to see things in a fixed way. That's the way we like it. Don't be like the shallow old husband who said, "I told my wife I loved her 40 years ago. If I change my mind, I'll let her know."

Once I was booked to perform on one of those three-hour-cruise boats. This is just a step up from performing at a Chuck-E-Cheese restaurant. Don't get me wrong. It's a wonderful boat, but it's not a cruise ship; you are surrounded by visual distractions. I was hired to do close-up magic. It takes years of practice to master close-up magic. The hardest part is getting the nerve to walk up to people who are in deep conversation and say, "Excuse me. Pick a card. Any card." I approached a nice lady. I said, "Hello, would you like to see some magic?" She answered, "No thanks. I just want to enjoy the view." She did not want to see magic. She wanted to see what she was already looking at, not what I wanted her to see. Not that I blame her. A sun disappearing beyond the horizon will trump a disappearing coin every time.

It's human nature to focus on what we *want* to see, but it can cause us to miss some of life's magic. In case you haven't noticed, this book is really about one main idea: *You will not experience the new life you want until you see things differently*. Marines say that pain is weakness leaving the body. But you and I are sub … marines. We tend to shrink from or sink into our difficulties. Our natural inclination is more along the lines of what Carol Leifer says is her philosophy of exercise: "No pain, no pain!"

But please get this: Your breakthrough will almost always come *after* (not before) you experience a breakdown. Sometimes you simply have to decide. Do you want to get better or get bitter?

I saw a woman wearing a sweatshirt with "Guess" on it.
I said, "Thyroid problem?"
—Emo Philips

Sometimes we need to hear bad news before we can accept the good news. A woman was sitting in the doctor's exam room. She was complaining about her condition. "Where is the doctor? I need to see the doctor!" A young nurse got tired of hearing the moaning so she walked into the exam room. After spending just a few minutes with the nurse, the poor patient ran out of the room screaming.

An older nurse stopped the woman and asked what the problem was. She had the patient sit down and try to relax. The older nurse then found the younger nurse and asked her, "What in the world were you thinking? Mrs. Johnson is 64 years old. She has four children and eight grandchildren. You told her she was *pregnant*?"

The young nurse smiled and said, "Yep. Sure cured her hiccups, didn't it?"

One night when I was single, I went out to dinner with a woman named Veronica. Like a real dating pro, I jumped right in with some fun casual conversation starters: religion, philosophy, and death.

I told Veronica that I struggled with depression. She excitedly told me about her favorite author. "She has written a wonderful book about beating depression and what she did to get over her own depression." Veronica told me about how this author had helped her and how the book really works when it comes to overcoming sadness. "That sounds great," I said. "I definitely want to check out that book. What's the author's name?" Veronica said, "Let me think, what was her name? Hmmm … I know she killed herself."

Take my advice ... please

That "expert" wasn't willing or able to take her own medicine. If you want to experience real change, you have to face the most difficult part of your core personal story. The pain point. You have to go to the place that hurts the most and find a new way of looking at it. I call this *re-framing through re-naming*. It's an ancient concept, going all the way back to the Bible. We see Abram become Abraham, Saul becomes Paul, and Jesus re-names Simon as Peter. New name. New identity.

I discovered the power of re-framing through re-naming when I was growing up. My parents named me Mark Duane Brown. My dad named me after Mark Twain, the great American humorist and author of *Tom Sawyer* and *Huckleberry Finn*. This was a real gift from my mom and dad. It has shaped my sense of self. Our personal names and nicknames can become our lenses on life. (Call your kid "stupid," but then don't be surprised if she acts the part.)

You can't have a simpler name than Mark Brown, can

you? I was already a joker in school, so I was called "Brown Clown." I didn't mind so much, and I never disliked my original name. It became confusing, however, during high school when another kid named Mark Brown arrived at the school. I was a senior, and he was a lowly freshman. It was my last year in high school. I was planning on enjoying the many privileges of being a senior. But right away I noticed something was funky. The school gave me a dreaded bottom locker. No way. What?

That bottom locker was meant for the other Mark Brown on campus. He got my top locker. Things went from bad to worse. I had always been an honor roll student, but when our first report cards came out, I got my new grades: D, C, D, D-, and F+. (Can you really get an "F+?" What is the + for? Breathing?) It was the other Mark Brown's report card, but it was given to me. He went home with my A's and B's.

This name mix-up kept happening. One day I came home and my mom was upset with me: "We just got a letter from the school. It says you have been expelled for getting into a fight. What happened?" It was the other Mark Brown, of course. A few years later I was married, and I got a call from the local police department. "We are looking for a Mark Brown." Turns out the other Mark Brown had stolen a six-pack of beer from a 7-11 convenience store. For the life of me, I couldn't understand how he turned out so badly since he always got such good grades in school.

By that time, however, I could laugh, because I had

changed my name to Adam Christing. It wasn't the hassles that made me do it. It was facing a crisis of doubt and pain. I suffered through the crisis and came out with a new point of view, a new sense of identity, and a new name. That name—Adam Christing—became more than a "stage name." It was my re-frame. I learned to see myself with an "A+" approval rating, not from parents, friends, or the police, but from God. It was a game-changer … and then a name-changer. Note: Nothing had changed for me in terms of circumstances, but I saw myself in a new way.

> *One's destination is never a place but rather,*
> *a new way of looking at things.*
> —Henry Miller

I saw my life in terms of new categories: guilt, grace, and then gratitude. And I discovered that these were not new ideas at all—they were actually the teachings of Saint Paul spelled out in his first century letter called *Romans*.

You don't have to legally change your name to change your perspective. But you must re-frame and re-name your biggest hardship so that it helps you become who you were meant to be. Remember the classic Christmas movie, *It's A Wonderful Life?* George Bailey is on the verge of losing everything. He is melting down. He has lashed out at his kids. His marriage is in trouble. He is flat broke and in danger of going to prison. It's not until his guardian angel allows him to see his life from a different perspective that George can re-frame his pain and celebrate his existence. His outer circumstances actually get worse (before they get better). But he now has a fresh outlook on life. One of the great moments of the film is when he says triumphantly, "Isn't it wonderful? I'm going to jail!"

That is the cry of a man who has listened, who has felt the pain, and who has come out the other side because he has learned to see things in a brand new way. What actually changed for George? Nothing. Yet everything! George got a new lens on life, and then he decided to re-frame his pain. You have a wonderful life, too. Do you see it that way?

AHA! Lesson #6

Re-frame your pain.

Questions to ask yourself as you laugh your way through the pain:

- Are you listening to what hurts?
- How do you see your pain?
- How could you re-frame it?

- Can you reconnect with an ancient truth to discover a new you?
- Can you re-tell your life story in a way where your pain is in the middle of your story and not the end of it?

7

YOUR WORK IS A JOKE

Let every man or woman here, if you never hear me again, remember this, that if you wish to be great at all, you must begin where you are and with what you are … now."
—Russell H. Conwell

Over the years, I have done a ton of comedy and speaking gigs. But I haven't come close to the record set by legendary speaker Russell Conwell back in the late 1800s. Conwell delivered one captivating speech "Acres of Diamonds" 6,152 times! Now, *there's* a guy who stayed on message.

He pulled this off before the invention of cars or Southwest airlines. The speech generated millions of dollars. Conwell funneled that money into his dream—building a college for underprivileged but deserving students. He raised nearly six million dollars—that's like 3.2 zillion dollars today. The university he founded, Temple University in Philadelphia, is still thriving today.

Conwell became famous as a lecturer. His message was delivered as part of a traveling tent show that visited towns in America's heartland, presenting musical performances, plays, political speeches, and spellbinding storytelling. Russell Conwell's "Acres of Diamonds" talk was part sermon, part drama, part stand-up comedy, and always entertaining. He never got tired of delivering his "Acres of Diamonds" message. Each time he shared it, he made it seem like it was the first time he had ever given the speech.

What was the main idea behind his famous speech?

Conwell told about a farmer who lived in Africa. The farmer was tired of farming—it was such tedious, hard work—and he became obsessed with the quest to find diamonds instead of raising turnips. Vast quantities of diamonds had been discovered on the African continent. This farmer was convinced that mining diamonds was a much better kind of work than digging turnips. He sold his farm. He left his family and friends and wandered all over the African desert.

Years slipped away. The poor farmer never found the diamonds he longed for. He ended up completely broke and miserable. He threw himself into a river and drowned.

Meanwhile, the new owner of his farm picked up an unusual looking rock and put it on his mantle as a conversation piece. A visitor came by, and when he saw the rock, he nearly fainted. He told the new owner of the farm that the crazy-looking rock on his mantle was a diamond. A very large diamond. It would, in fact, prove to be the biggest diamond that had ever been discovered. The new owner of the farm said, "Really? The whole farm is covered with them."—and indeed it was.

The farm turned out to be the Kimberly Diamond Mine ... the richest diamond mine the world has ever known. The original farmer was literally standing right on top of his own "Acres of Diamonds."

It's right under your nose!

The point is that each of us is right in the middle of our own "Acre of Diamonds" right where we are now.

Magicians are known for closely guarding secrets. How do we do it? Some magicians say, "The best way to hide a secret … is to put it in print." The idea is that people don't notice what's in plain sight. Here's a true story about a magician friend of mine: Dana Daniels is an award-winning comedy magician. He does a hilarious act with Luigi … his "psychic parrot."

Back before 9/11, when you could actually get through airport security without having to undergo a colonoscopy, Dana wanted to save the hassle of traveling with Luigi in a birdcage. So, he resorted to smuggling. He thought it would be a fun challenge. Dana hid Luigi in his inside coat pocket.

When Dana checked in at the baggage counter, the ticket agent looked at him and said, "One bag to check in?" Dana said, "Yes, sir." The man then asked, "You want to check in the parrot?" Dana thought, *How does he know I have a parrot? Did he see my show last night?* He was bewildered, so he thought he'd just blow it off and said "What parrot?" The ticket agent looked up at him and said, "The one on your shoulder."

While he was waiting in line, Luigi had crawled out of his pocket and up onto his shoulder. He had no idea how long he'd been there. Dana assumed that humor was the only way out of this situation, so he said with a straight face, "No, he's here to see me off." The guy cracked up, then handed him his ticket and said, "Here you go, Mr. Daniels."

If you're looking for a helping hand,
there's one at the end of your arm.
—Jewish proverb

Your life is a joke. Make sure you "get it." Something very important for you may be hidden in plain sight. Your best opportunities are right in your own backyard. The big "break" you are looking for ... the job you really want ... the love you are seeking ... the extra income you need ...

the friends who will care about you … it's ALL right under your nose.

One day I was rushing off to the airport to catch a flight. I couldn't find my cell phone. I was hunting everywhere for it, while talking to my friend about it ... *on my cell phone.*

We tend to look everywhere else for what we already have in hand.

My wife and I took a bunch of nine-year-old boys to the movies for my son James' birthday party. On the ride home his best friend Ryan suddenly burst into tears. "Oh no! I left my iPod in the movie theater!" Are you kidding me? We were almost home and guests were waiting for us at our house. We called Ryan's mom and left her a message, "You need to go to the movie theater. Ryan left his iPod there!" We called the theater and (after listening to the recording of the eighteen movie screenings,) asked the manager to search our seats. "Please help us find this little boy's treasured electronic device." Ryan was in the car, crying. The kids felt it was an emergency. WE MUST FIND RYAN'S iPod.

We pulled into the driveway, got out of the car, and Ryan instantly stopped crying. He said, "Oh. Cool. It was right here in my back pocket."

What's in *your* back pocket? Who is *already* in your address book? What opportunities are awaiting you—in your own backyard?

As the wise philosopher, Justin Bieber, once sang, "The

grass is greener … where you water it." When you notice, choose and cultivate what you have, something powerful happens. Your attention moves from looking for what's "out there" to realizing that *what you are looking for is right here.*

I wondered why the baseball was getting bigger. Then it hit me

Often it's a matter of how you see things. If someone asks me what I do and I say, "I tell jokes," people tend to smile politely and nod—no doubt thinking that I'm some kind of part-time clown who does bad stand-up in the local bar on open mic Fridays. If, however, I say, "I'm a comedian who delivers inspiration, motivation and life lessons to corporate clients all over the world," suddenly I'm a *big deal.* I'm someone whose brain they might want to pick. I'm someone whom they may want to hire. I'm someone who can make more than balloon animals. Suddenly, I can make a difference.

Just as with a joke, it's all in the set-up, or the hook, or the way you position yourself—*and you are 100 percent in charge of this part of your work life.*

It's easier to ask forgiveness than it is to get permission.
—Grace Hopper
(she was the oldest serving officer
in the United States Navy)

Give yourself the permission you are seeking

One of the transforming realizations I had in my business life was that *you don't have to wait for someone else to give you permission.* You can make a declaration about yourself. When my friend, the great pantomime artist Cary Trivanovich gave me the idea that morphed into my company *Clean Comedians*, I took action immediately. (Note: Sure, it was tempting to insert a mime joke here. Heck, a mime is a terrible thing to waste. But I resisted.)

I got a business license. And here's the thing: I declared myself the "president" of the organization. Let me be clear. There was no election. I named myself the president of a company that only existed in my heart and imagination. My dad helped a little when he suggested that my original title, "Supreme Dictator For Life," sounded a little too extreme. Since that time, *Clean Comedians* has booked nearly two hundred entertainers and speakers into thousands of meetings and events. I have been introduced on many radio and TV shows as "the president of *Clean Comedians*." It's a pretty great punch line.

Remember that I was just a kid who started out with a business card that said, "Magic for All Occasions." My work back then really *was* a joke—because I didn't see the opportunities that were there waiting for me to just reach down and retrieve them. I didn't see that my love of comedy, my passion for comedy, and my drive to do comedy, were diamonds in the rough. Comedy and magic were just things I liked and things I did. Now, however, I see things in a whole new light. I see that I was standing on "Acres of Diamonds" all along. My work is rewarding. Every time I perform, I feel like I am doing some good in the world. And I can now splurge on the $18 cotton candy at Disneyland that my son loves. I can buy the $1,200 braces my daughter needs. And just last month, I bought an 8-track of *Frampton Comes Alive* at a garage sale just because I wanted it.

Like I said—I have a pretty fun punch line. Do you? If not, look closely at what is right in front of you and give yourself permission to pursue it.

Entertainers know that while someone may book them, and someone may call them up to the stage, they are the only person who can give them permission to *own* that stage. A great joke will fall flat as a pancake if the comedian doesn't own it. A comedian's "Acres of Diamonds" lie in his ability to be confident, and to give himself permission to seize the power in the room.

Many smart business people have made fortunes simply by seeing the opportunity in front of them and seizing it. In the not-so-old days, TV news was a very sober affair. Peter Jennings would sit there and stoically tell the world what was happening, and we would all listen because that was the way the news was delivered. In the mid '90s however, Jon Stewart got the brilliant idea that news was actually hilarious. If looked at in the right way, news could be fodder for all kinds of jokes. Jon soon found that people would rather hear their news in this fresh, new way than in the stodgy old way. *The Daily Show* was born. Jon Stewart gave himself permission to see the news as funny. He looked at what was right in front of him—*the news is funny!*—and seized the chance to make something of it. Oh, by the way, Jon Stewart? Not his original name. It's the name taken by a guy named Jonathan Leibowitz who wanted to re-frame himself.

I've always loved the story (actually I am making it up right now) of the scientist who held up a large sheet of paper and made one black dot in the center. He asked his lab assistants, "What do you see?" Each of them agreed with the others and said, "I see the black dot." The scientist said, "You nerds have all overlooked the biggest thing—the sheet of paper!"

Don't miss the opportunities right under your nose. Ever hear about the guy who did carpentry work for a film director? It was the work that was in front of him to do, and it also became his "Acres of Diamonds." He ended up with the chance to read for the director and Harrison Ford landed the role of "Han Solo" in a movie you may have heard about, called *Star Wars*.

Your work is a joke. Look closely at the opportunities and resources right under your nose. Decide what you want your punch line to be, and take action to see and enjoy your own "Acres of Diamonds."

AHA! Lesson #7

Do what's in front of you.

Questions to ask yourself when you can't see the forest for the trees:

- What could you see, right in your own backyard, that is in fact what you need to work on?
- What work opportunities are you currently sitting on? How can you take action to claim them?
- What do you need to give yourself permission to do?
- How can you maximize the resources and relationships you already have?
- What are you doing instead of what you should be doing when it comes to work?

8

YOUR MONEY IS A JOKE

Money makes a wonderful servant,
but a terrible master.
—P.T. Barnum

Over the last few decades I have earned several million dollars. But like those magical sponge bunnies, my money has appeared in my hands, multiplied, and then disappeared. What happened to my money? I could blame the economy. I could blame the speaking or entertainment biz. But I choose to blame my mom instead. She was my company treasurer. She's currently serving a ten-year sentence for embezzlement.

I'm kidding! She's wonderful and has been my biggest

fan. She's always made me feel that I could do great things. But I mistakenly took to heart, deep inside of me, an off-hand comment she said about me many years ago. I over-heard her talking on the phone to someone and heard her say, "He's never been good with money." Of the zillions of things I could choose to believe, of all the positive things she has said to or about me, I let *that* thought take root in my head. *That's right. I've never been good with money.*

What we believe to be true about ourselves—our set-up—creates our "personal punch line," our experience of life. Well, "bad with money" has been an ongoing premise and recurring experience in my life. When I went through my divorce, it was due in large part to the way I handled (or didn't handle) money. I knew how to make it, but not how to manage it. It's like I feel that it's not really mine or that I'm not entitled to it. And I don't blame my mom. I take responsibility for this.

You think you have money problems. You don't. You have one money problem, the same money problem over and over again. *The way you handle money is the way you handle life.*

One of the most important relationships in your life is your relationship with money. Money doesn't make you who you are, but it sure reveals what you are. Your net worth does not equal your self worth. But money does show you what you value. And *the way you handle money is the way you handle life.* It's time you show your money who's boss.

Money doesn't make you ... money reveals you

A lawyer was walking out of a store at Christmas time. He heard the sound of a ringing bell. He saw a Salvation Army worker who said to him, "Hello Sir, would you like to make a donation to help a local family in need?" The lawyer said, "Do you realize that *my* mother is dying, and her medical bills are piling up?" The Salvation Army volunteer replied, "Oh, no. I'm very sorry to hear that."

The lawyer said, "Did you happen to know that *my* sister's husband lost his job, and *my* nieces and nephews won't be getting any toys this Christmas?" The Salvation Army worker replied, "I'm terribly sorry." The lawyer continued, "And *my* secretary's house just burnt to the ground, and her family has no insurance. Her family is now penniless." The Salvation Army volunteer was on the verge of tears and said, "I'm so sorry to hear all this." As the lawyer walked away, he scoffed, "I don't help any of them, so why should I give money to you?"

There are tons of lawyer jokes. The shortest one I know is this:

Q: What do you call a lawyer with an I.Q. of 50?

A: "Your Honor!"

Remember that you have a funny way of looking at money, too. To improve your relationship with money, *you first must understand how you relate to money*. What outcome do you get from your income? Do you deal with debt or does debt deal with you? Do you think of yourself as a saver or a misbehaver? There are three main money mindsets, and of course, they rhyme: the locker, rocker, and knocker. I will outline them for you below. You'll be able to spot your mindset right away.

When you're in a hole, stop digging.
—Abraham Lincoln

Before I explain them, let me make one thing clear: None of the following money mindsets are right or wrong. I'm not telling you to change your money mindset. You can't. They call it "personal finances" for a reason. It's personal. Very. I'm not encouraging you to change who you are. I'm encouraging you to identify which one of these money mindsets best describes you and then to build on the best aspects of that mindset.

TYPE ONE: If you are a LOCKER, you see money as safety.

I have enough money to last me the rest of my life—unless I buy something.
—Jackie Mason

The following joke captures the money mindset of a "locker."

Three men were sentenced to death. On the day they were

to suffer their fate, the judge tells them: "You can choose the method of your execution. Would you prefer to die by lethal injection or the electric chair?"

The first man chooses lethal injection. He is injected and dies. The second guy gets the same choice: "Lethal injection or electric chair?" He chooses the electric chair. They strap him to the chair, but when they pull the switch nothing happens. They pull the switch again. Still, nothing happens! The judge says, "Well, according to the law, the death penalty was administered to you. There's nothing more that we can do to you. You are free to go." The man goes free.

The judge calls up the third man: "You are the final execution of the day. Lethal injection or electric chair?" The man says, "Definitely lethal injection. The electric chair is obviously broken." Poor guy. So focused on micromanaging, he didn't see that he could go free.

Cheap, cheap, cheap

Jack Benny was one of the greatest comedians of the 20th century. He got one of the biggest laughs in the history of both radio and television. And it was all *based on his joke set-up*. Benny was a "locker." He was cheap.

When a robber held him up at gunpoint and said, "Your money or your life?" Jack Benny paused (for what seemed like the longest and funniest silence ever) and finally said,

"I'm thinking ... I'm thinking."

If you have the money mindset of a "locker," and you like to hold on to your money, that can be a good thing. Jack Benny became a very wealthy man. Just make sure you enjoy it and laugh your way to the bank.

Dangers for "lockers" include the following:

- Not enjoying the gift of giving
- Not maximizing potential earnings
- Not feeling the freedom to enjoy money

The Bottom Line: If you are a "locker," you can maximize your relationship with money by reframing the idea of spending and giving. Think of it as helping to secure a stable future for those you care about.

TYPE TWO: If you are a ROCKER, you see money as fun.

I can't be out of money ... I still have checks!
—Seen on a T-shirt

Rockers want what they want and don't want to wait for it. They want to have their cake, eat it now, and pay for it later.

A man went into a cake shop and said, "I want a beautiful cake shaped like the letter K." The cake maker said, "No problem, Sir. Why don't you come back this afternoon at 3:00, and we'll have it ready for you."

When the man returned to the cake shop, the baker

showed him the cake. The man said, "No, no. I don't want it to look like a printed K, I want it cursive style, like a signature. The baker tells him, "Oh, we can do that for you. Just come back at 6:00 tonight, and we'll have it baked just right for you." The man returns at 6:00. He loves the cake, but he says, "This is great, but I want different frosting. Can you do it with only yellow and blue frosting?"

The baker tells him, "Sure, but we'll need at least 30 minutes." The man comes back a half hour later. "It's perfect!" The cake baker is relieved. He starts to put the cake in a box for the man. But the man says, "No, you don't need to do that. I'll eat it here."

Rockers want to taste what their money can buy them *now.* If you have the money mindset of a "rocker," that's okay. You realize that money (and life) is to be enjoyed. Just make sure you "enjoy responsibly."

Dangers for "rockers" include:

- No written budget
- Tax problems
- Borrow today = sorrow tomorrow

The Bottom Line: If you are a "rocker," you can maximize your relationship with money by re-framing savings and investments as a new and exciting form of spending.

TYPE THREE: If you are a KNOCKER, you see money as opportunity, and you will spend money to make more money.

Buy low. Sell high. Pay late. Collect early.
—Anonymous

Years ago, I bumped into a street performer named Mikey in downtown San Francisco. He was a fabulous juggler. He set up his gear and his tip jar in the business district, about 20 feet away from a Bank of America. I asked him why he wasn't working near Fisherman's Wharf or Pier 39 where most street performers work. He told me, "I like to entertain people while they're waiting in line for the ATM, because that's where the money's at!"

Money is funny

One time I produced a comedy concert in Orange County, California. It was pretty unheard of to land this particular engagement. This club mostly books used-to-be-famous rock bands. I was a start-up comedian at the time, but I booked myself and several other entertainers at this theater and saw my name and the names of my funny friends up on the marquee. How did I get this gig? It was easy. I rented the place. When I went to the club manager's office, my intent was to "pitch" the big show for the club and have them pay for it. But I realized immediately that there was a faster way to get my name in lights with this venue. The manager actually had a giant sign on the wall for people to see when they sat down to talk with him. The sign said: WE WANT MONEY. Once I realized that this club owner worshipped the almighty buck, I knew how to speak his language. I am a "knocker."

If you are a "knocker," don't knock it. You have a mindset that, like the other money mindsets, can lead to success. If you can manage your tendency to take risks, you can manage your money, and lots of it.

Dangers for "knockers" could include:

- Postponing feelings of worth and well-being
- Not being protected from economic downturns
- Scaring loved ones who are security-minded

The Bottom Line: If you are a "knocker," you can maximize your relationship with money through careful research and wise investments.

Make a lot. Save a lot. Give a lot.
—Phil Liberatore, The IRS Problem Solver

No matter how much money you make or have, don't let it have you. When the world's first billionaire, John D. Rockefeller was asked, "Mr. Rockefeller, how much money is enough?" Rockefeller joked back: "A little bit more." Happily for him and others, he spent the second half of his life giving away his massive fortune.

You may not feel wealthy today. But if you look at human history, guess what? You are incredibly rich. Water? Turn on the faucet. Food? Open the fridge. Medical problem? Dial

9-1-1. You and I have privileged problems.

The secret to happiness is not making money, or even saving it. The big secret is generous giving. Don't be a taker, be a giver. Don't wait to give until you have a lot. Because if you don't give now, you won't give then. When you give now, you will have a lot … of great feelings, of lasting joy, and of the deep knowledge that you are living a meaningful life.

The way you spend (or don't spend) your money is the way you spend your life. This is a book about you creating a personal paradigm shift. I'm heading out now to have lunch with my wonderful mom. I am going to give her a card of thanks for all she has done and continues to do for me. And I am having her sign her name to a 3 x 5 card that I'll keep in my wallet that says, "My son is fantastic with money!" I'm changing my set-up about money. You can, too.

AHA! Lesson #8

Show your money who's boss.

Questions to ask yourself when you feel broke … but not broken:

- Which money type are you?
- How does this mindset hurt you?
- What positive aspect of your money type can help you if you cultivate it?
- How can you make the most of your money mindset?
- What causes can you support that have great meaning to you?

9

YOUR RELATIONSHIPS ARE A JOKE

I have a detached retina.
Actually, it's not detached, it's emotionally unavailable.
—Nick Arnette

One night before going on stage to perform my comedy show, I was doing what magicians call "table-hopping" —demonstrating close-up magic from group to group. I was at a country club. I was performing a cool little card trick—a classic one that can give people the impression of real mind reading—though it's actually just an illusion.

The reaction at one of the tables was fantastic. "NO WAY. THAT'S IMPOSSIBLE! HOW COULD YOU KNOW WHAT CARD I WAS THINKING OF? HEY, CAN YOU

MAKE MY HUSBAND DISAPPEAR?" Some of these people were drinking a lot of wine. (This always makes the magic far more amazing.) The reactions I was getting from that card trick were good.

But the reaction that blew *me* away came from a normal-looking 35-year-old woman. When I was finished with the mind reading card trick, she stood up from the table and followed me to the next table. "I need a reading," she whispered, "Please give me a reading." By that, she meant a "psychic" reading. She wanted me to tell her about her future. I guess it wasn't an enormous stretch to think that I could give her mystical guidance. After all, when a trick "kills" in a big way, magicians like to say, "You could start a religion with *that*."

"Oh, thank you," I told her, "But what I showed you was just a magic trick … you know … sleight of hand, an illusion. I don't have powers." But she wouldn't give up.

"I know you can see things," she said with increasing urgency, "I really need you to give me a reading." Finally, I gave in. I pretended to be psychic. But I used my "powers" for good.

ME: I'm sensing … are you struggling with a relationship right now?

WOMAN: There is NO way you could have known that!

ME: I'm seeing that you need to make an important

decision about this relationship. Is that right?

WOMAN: Yes. I can't even believe you know this somehow. Yes. Yes.

ME: This time, you need to do the right thing. Don't you?

WOMAN (now crying): Wow. I can't even believe this. Yes, that's right. Oh … thank you, thank you.

I took this opportunity to make myself vanish. While she was sobbing and going on about what she needed to do, I hid behind a fake Roman decorative pillar on the grounds. When she turned around to look for me, I snuck behind the portable curtains on the platform to get ready for my stage show.

I didn't want her to look to me for more details on the meaning she needed. She already knew what she needed to do. She just needed to experience a relation*shift*. I hope she did.

How did I guess the woman was struggling with a relationship? It wasn't rocket science. She had a pulse. I could tell she was in pain, and if you're in pain, you need to make a decision that will alleviate that pain, not just cover it up.

Now you see me

The truth is we all struggle with relationships. *The things that are most meaningful in your life are connected to your relationships.* To make them better, *you* must shift your own perception. It's an inside job. If you don't change the way YOU look at your part in a relationship, you will keep getting hurt. You need to get closer to people ... in a healthy way. You need a relation*shift*.

It reminds me of a prank I used to pull—a mean one I'm not proud of—when I was in junior high school. I'd walk up to a kid and say, "Hey, come close, let's have a contest. Let's see which one of us can hit the other guy the *softest*. Okay? Ready ... you go first." The other kid would barely punch my arm. I could hardly feel it. And then, *wham*. I would punch him super hard on the shoulder and say, "Ha Ha. You win!"

We can find ourselves in relationships that seem close, but set us up for pain. When we expect someone else to do something like we want it done, we are going to get disappointed. Expectations are planned disappointments. You have to keep your focus on what you can control. That woman at the country club was looking outside herself. She was looking to me, for one thing—which was clearly crazy. And she was also no doubt hoping that her boyfriend would magically change. We all do this. You and I mistakenly think that our parents, our partner, our coworkers, our kids, and our customers are going to one day just magically transform themselves into someone else. *Then* (we think) things will get better for us. But we end up getting hurt, because the other person isn't a puppet on a string. It's a bad set-up.

There are things you can do to experience close

relationships, but it comes back to how you look at things. This reminds me of a classic story about an older man who bought his first cell phone:

> *MAN (to his wife):* Honey, I'm calling you from the freeway on my new cell phone.
> *WIFE:* Well be careful, George. I just saw a news flash on TV about a crazy guy driving on the wrong side of the highway.
> *MAN:* One crazy guy? Are you kidding? I see tons of them!

After we get hit a few times, we become guarded. "I'll start acting nice when he starts being nice to me." "I'll show them respect when they start respecting me." Your life is a joke. Make sure you set it up right with the other characters in your story. Notice a pattern? It all goes back to your set-up. You are sending out a billion little signals to the world about who you are, what people should call you, and how they should treat you. Shift those signals, shift your own direction, and you shift your relationships into positive gear.

All alone together

One night, when my daughter, Katie was five-years-old, she and I were sitting in the family room. Nobody else was home.

She looked at me excited and said, "Hey Daddy, we're all alone together!" Out of the mouths of babes often comes … cereal. But her observation was pure gold. We are alone. But we are alone in this world together.

Your best memories of busting up and laughing your head off—laughing so hard you couldn't stop—are always connected to experiencing that bliss of busting up *along with someone else*. Laughing together is the best kind of laughter. Victor Borge once said, "A smile is the shortest distance between two people."

Your life gets better when you get closer to people. Here are some strategies from the world of comedy that can help you in your relationships:

The secret strategy of comedy clubs is not the alcohol. It's this:

They create a feeling of intimacy in the audience. They pack people in and seat them super close to each other. This makes the laughter feel contagious.

A physical gap between the comedian and crowd kills the connection. A dance floor between my audience and me feels like the Grand Canyon. I tell event coordinators who book me to move the chairs closer to the stage and get people closer to each other. I tell them, "The closer *they* get, the funnier *I* get."

The secret strategy of great comedians
is not vulgarity… it's vulnerability.

Many people think that Howard Stern gained his popularity by being crude. Not so. He became a big celebrity by being incredibly transparent about his life. Stern once said, "To get to the next level you have to open up a lot more." It goes back to intimacy. Here's an interesting way of looking at that word:

Intimacy = Into Me See

Headliners open up

I have four kids. That means I have lots of stories. My oldest son, Randy is a professional poker player and a master of bluffing. But when he was just three-years-old, he taught me about the power of total transparency. I was about to drive off to do a gig at a college when suddenly Randy came darting out of the front door of the house. He was wearing only his Batman underpants, and he was crying. I stopped the engine of my car and got out. He ran to me, and with tears in his eyes, he sobbed, "Daddy, I didn't get to hug you goodbye!" So what did I do? Naturally, I spanked him. No way. I lifted him up in my arms. I gave him a big hug and told him that I loved him.

When my little boy came running to me he wasn't guarded. He spoke from his heart, not his head. He didn't say, "Father, we need to discuss the level of affection in our relationship." He was direct, "Dad, I want a hug." *He got what he wanted because he shared what he needed.*

What are you openly asking for in your relationships? Are you letting others see your feelings? If you want to deepen your relationship, don't close off. Open up. Become more vulnerable.

Randy has graduated from college. He's in his mid-twenties now. I still feel close to him. Every year we go on a trip where we can hang out together. We share experiences and our thoughts and feelings, and he crushes me in B-ball. It's one of my favorite parts of the year. Give each of your kids quality one-on-one time. They will remember it for the rest of their lives. Every relationship you are in—with your spouse, your kids, your clients—needs connection time.

What is the secret of humor?

The secret of humor is not happiness ... it's hurt.

I was once asked to contribute to a book on *How to Increase Your Creativity*. The editor asked dozens of professional comedians to submit their sources for creating humor. I mailed him a sheet of paper with my name and one word on it: *Pain*. The best comedians, the best writers, the best communicators, are the people who truly empathize with our pain. You might think that people want you to do things for them. And sometimes that's true. But *what they really care about is how you make them feel.*

The world is asking only one question:
"Can you help me where I hurt?"
—Pastor Orval C. Butcher

The comedian's secret to connecting with a crowd is: Engage the audience while detaching from hecklers.

I love to tell jokes. But the biggest laughs I get come from my audience participation and spontaneous interaction with a group. I use audience members throughout my show. I usually get a very strong round of applause, and frequently a standing ovation, at the end of my performance. You know why? I treat the audience members as "co-stars" in my show. And they feel it too. I conclude my set by saying, "I couldn't have done it tonight without my co-stars. How about a big hand for: Mike, Tim, Melanie, Fernando, of course Brittany … and let's not forget Robert or Stephanie. My name is Adam Christing, good night!" APPLAUSE. It's not about me. It's about we.

The best comedians know how to disengage from hecklers.

Remember the country club lady I told you about? The one who wanted a "reading." What she really wanted was permission to get out of a bad relationship. She had a husband or a boyfriend who was like a "heckler"

—disrupting her mojo, disrespecting her, making it impossible for her to connect. There are only two ways you can handle the "hecklers" in your life. You can either put up with them or put them down … and out.

One time I was giving a lecture to a bunch of magicians. Steve Barnes was in the audience. He is hilarious. He was heckling me. I would hit him back with a vintage heckler put-down (something like: "I wouldn't go to your job and unplug the Slurpee machine.") But he kept coming back and cracking everybody up. After about 10 volleys back and forth it dawned on me. "This is more fun *with* him than against him." I played into Steve's antics, and the crowd loved it. Bonus note: Steven Barnes is still at it. He agreed to support my Kickstarter book campaign ... if I included a story about him. I just did.

Look for win/win scenarios like that. But sometimes you have to stop a heckler in his or her tracks. If somebody is ruining your performance, you have to quiet them down, make them look ridiculous, or get them booed out of the room.

When I get heckled, I quickly remember three things:

1. It's my show.
2. The audience is on my side.
3. I have the microphone.

Apply this to your life. First, it's *your* life. Second, there are people who care about you. Third, you can control what you say and who you choose to listen to.

It's all about connecting

Here's what matters: Keep the connection with your core audience and *disconnect from the detractors in your life.*

I found nothing really wrong with this autobiography except poor choice of subject.
—Clifton Fadiman

How do you disconnect? I'm writing this chapter from a hotel room in Dallas, Texas. I just ended a bad relationship with a cab driver. Fortunately, it was only a two-minute relationship. It started after I flew from LAX to Albuquerque, to Dallas. I grabbed my suitcase, my bag of tricks, and my computer bag. When I got curbside I noticed that there were 27 cabs, and I was supposed to get into the one that was at the front of the line.

I put my bags into the guy's cab. But when I told him where my hotel was, he refused to take me there. I said, "And why is that?" He said, "It's too close. It's not worth it to me." I couldn't believe it. I considered for a moment arguing with the guy, making a stink, calling over the supervisor who was prowling the sidewalk. Instead, I disengaged. I calmly got out of the cab, pulled all of my bags out of the trunk. I was upset—don't get me wrong—and while this doesn't always happen, this time justice was served, and I had the last laugh. The airport cab supervisor saw what happened and told the cab driver. "Go. Get out of here! Nobody is going to ride with you now." So the guy drove off. Turns out, this driver waited three hours in line at the airport to get his turn at the front of the line. It was bad luck that I was only offering a three-mile trip. But as Willy Wonka once said when he was upset with Grampa Joe, "You lose! You get *nothing*! Good day, sir!"

Because he was not willing to deal with a close drive, he got no ride, no tip, nothing. That driver ended up booed by the other cabbies. And I became an honorary member of the cab community that night, which felt awesome. When I need a lift, these are my people.

Comedians can't work without an audience. And *your life doesn't work when you are in isolation* and not connected with others. Now get this point. It's a biggie. When people talk about great comedians or entertainers, they often say, "Wow, he has great timing." What they really mean is that the great performer is a fantastic listener. You can *listen* your way into better relationships far better than you can talk your way into them.

Talk to people about themselves and they will listen for hours.
—Benjamin Disraeli

My actor/comedian friend Randy McDowell made me laugh talking about the way technology is affecting our communications. He says that when somebody sends you a text you say, "Cool! What is it?" When you get an email you think, "What do they want?" When you get a phone call your reaction is, "Who died?"

Technology today has us confusing faster with closer. Don't fall for it. Connecting is not just "sending." It is listening. In-person time and talking/listening on the phone is far more powerful and meaningful than one-way messaging—but it requires more time and emotional investment. One of the ways I boosted my career and my bookings was by doing something ancient: *Meeting with people in person.* I took my cue here from Jay Leno. It was multiple in-person meetings that landed Leno on the *Tonight Show* when David Letterman appeared to be the successor to Johnny Carson. Leno took the time to meet with TV executives face to face and on the phone. He listened to them. He got the big gig.

Relation*shifts* happen when you are sitting together with someone. So take your mom to lunch. Hold hands while you walk in the park with your spouse. Tell your kids a story while they are sitting on your lap. Play a board game instead of a video game. And if you decide to play Monopoly, by all means get the Orange properties. You will wipe everybody out … in a loving way, of course.

Draw your family, your friends, your associates, your personal audience TOGETHER.

AHA! Lesson #9

Closer together makes it better.

Questions to ask yourself when your kids want to know if you're there yet:

- What do you need to change about you (instead of waiting for someone else to improve)?
- Who do you want to get closer to?
- How can you be more vulnerable with others (while still being wise)?
- What have you been holding inside that you could open up about?
- Who is your core "audience"?
- Can you exchange fast technology time for meaningful connection time? How? When?
- Who are the hecklers in your life that you can detach from? Will you?

10

YOUR DEATH IS A JOKE

Thank you for flying with us. Have a great day ...
wherever your final destination may take you.
—Southwest Airlines Flight Attendant

Death destroys your body. But the idea of death can transform your life.

Family and friends sometimes ask me to "officiate" (be the guest minister) at the funerals of dear ones who have died. Why do they ask me to do this? It's not because I put "Funerals Can Be Fun!"on my new business cards. Maybe it's because I get the joke: Life is the intersection of comedy and tragedy. Franz Kafka said, "The meaning of life is that it stops." Hmmm. But does it? Bob Dylan once sang in that sweet voice of his, "Just remember that death is not the end."

Death makes up ponder our purpose

I always say yes to the funeral gigs because it's nice to be a caring voice, but also because it's the ultimate reminder that life is short, and YES, I am still alive. I have noticed something fascinating about how we behave when somebody dies. On the way to the service, and during the funeral, everybody cries. But on the way home, everybody laughs. That's how it should be. You can only stand around at the graveside for so long before somebody says, "Hey, where should we go for lunch?"

You must begin to see yourself as a finite, temporary, mortal creature. You will have a more meaningful time on earth when you realize that *you are running out of time, even if you live to be 128.* I want you to have the last laugh while you are still living. Don't wait to celebrate.

What are your beliefs about the afterlife? You may find peace of mind by believing in heaven, a return visit to earth, or from the philosopher Epicurus who encouraged his students to remember that, "When life is, death is not. When death is, life is not." (I'm sure his pupils said, "How awesome! Wait ... what?") *But this chapter is not about what happens after death, it's about what happens to you when you are alive.*

The way you look at death matters. This classic joke illustrates how your perspective about living affects the quality of your life.

One day the Pope died. When he arrived in Heaven, Saint Peter was there to greet him. Peter embraced him and said, "Welcome to Heaven! My job is to make your first day here wonderful. Is there anything I can show you? Anything you'd like to see now that you are here in paradise?"

The Pope thought about it for a second and said, "Wow. Do you have the original Bible? I'd love to read the very first copy of the Holy Book." Peter said, "Of course. I'll be right back." When he returned, Saint Peter had the original manuscript of the Bible. He escorted the Pope to a private reading room, handed the Scriptures to him, and said, "Here you go, brother. Enjoy. I will be back in a couple of hours to see if I can get you anything else." The Pope was thrilled. He began to read page after page of the original Bible.

Saint Peter returned two hours later to find the Pope weeping uncontrollably, his index finger pointing right in the middle of the text. Saint Peter said, "What's wrong?"

The Pope looked up at him. "The word was cele*brate* … "

You can best celebrate your life when you contemplate your passing. The quality of your life hinges upon the *realization of your own death.* Sounds fun, I know. Here's when *it* first hit me. I was seven-years-old, in the second grade. I was walking—no, come to think of it, I was skipping along—at Edison elementary school. I was headed to the playground when it dawned on me. It hit me. I stopped right there in my tracks. I was just a kid, but the realization shot through my entire 58-pound being: *One. Day. I. Will. Die. Too.*

My mother had just returned from a funeral in Colorado. It was the first time I had even heard about a family member dying. My saint-like great-grandmother Frances had passed away. Like a joke that goes over your head, I didn't really get what it all meant. And that morning at school, as a little boy, I suddenly felt it in my gut like a revelation. *Wait, if great-grandma could die, so will I. This is going to happen to me one day, too.* I was frozen in my tracks. A minute later, I started walking, and soon I was back to skipping around with my friends—but I wasn't quite as carefree. The worst possible thing you could ever imagine *was* true. Death had dawned on me.

Inconceivable

In our heads we know that death is inevitable, but that's not how it feels in our hearts. It feels unacceptable. We think of ourselves as logical beings. As kids, we learn simple math formulas like 2+2=4. As we get older, we learn about deductive reasoning.

PREMISE 1: Socrates is a man
PREMISE 2: All men are mortal
CONCLUSION: Therefore, Socrates is mortal

This kind of thinking makes perfect sense, but when it comes to our own mortality, it just doesn't sound right. It can't be. But it makes sense …

PREMISE 1: All living things die
PREMISE 2: I am a living thing
CONCLUSION: Therefore, I will die

When faced with this reality, we start looking for outs. Maybe there was a misprint. You can't always trust logic anyway, right? I mean, what about this "logical" sequence?

PREMISE 1: Love is blind
PREMISE 2: Marriage is an institution
CONCLUSION: Marriage is an institution for the blind

In our heart of hearts, the notion of our own death feels to us like what William Saroyan, the brilliant dramatist who wrote *The Human Comedy,* told the press a few days before he passed away, "Everybody has to die, but I always believed an exception would be made in my case. Now what?" Notice his last two words: *Now what?* He was getting at another question: “How should I live in light of the fact that I'm going to die?” Sadly, he only had a few days to meditate on that question so we didn’t get to hear his answer. Hopefully, you have more time than that, but the truth is that very few of us actually get to the “Now what?” part.

Life was a funny thing that happened to me
on the way to the grave.
—Quentin Crisp

It’s crucial that you face up to the fact of death so you can maximize the quality and impact of your life while the clock is still ticking. *You need to attend your own funeral long before your body does.* We cheat ourselves out of a deeper experience of living because of our denial of death. We miss the magic of *being alive* when we buy into the illusion that this road trip will never end. Bestselling authors pump out dozens of near-death books. Make sure you don’t have a “near-life” experience.

Your life is structured like a joke. It has a beginning (your set-up), a middle (your setbacks), and an end (surprise!). As Robin Williams said, “Death is nature’s way of saying … *Your table’s ready*.” At the height of Steve Martin’s fame as a stand-up comic, he would say, “We’ve had a good time tonight, considering we’re all going to *die*.”

Some people grapple with it, but find death so repulsive that they lash out and take an angry stand against God. Like the philosopher Friedrich Nietzsche, who wanted to transcend death … to become the "over-man" or superman. It didn't work out too well for poor Friedrich.

In 1886 Nietzsche said, "God is dead."

In 1900 God said, "Nietzsche is dead."

Not sure why the first three letters of funeral are FUN. But I will say this, you can have more fun when you realize that life is a present to be opened and enjoyed. I have religious friends who want to skip ahead and not really come to grips with the reality of death. Some say, "It's nothing much. It's just like sleep." Are you ready for your wake-up call?

My Hindu friends say, "I believe in reincarnation." It's tempting to say, "Welcome back." A lot of Christians say, "Don't worry, you will go to Heaven." And many of them think that we are living in the last days and won't even experience death because Jesus will beam believers up into the sky while others are left behind. But the shortest verse in the Bible contains two words: "Jesus wept." He had heard that his friend Lazarus had died. Think about that one. In that story, Jesus later raises Lazarus from the dead. But when he heard about his friend's passing, he didn't say, "Hey, no worries. He'll be back with us pretty quick. Chill out." No, he cried. As lyricist Terry Scott Taylor has said, "Before he danced, Jesus wept." Death is real. And death is sad. Death is as certain as life. So … now what?

Whatever you believe about the afterlife, it's important to recognize—in the deepest level of yourself—that your earthly life is only good for a limited time. We all know this. But we don't live like it. Our "set-up" tells us that life goes on. Funerals bring us back to the fact: This life ends. So you must answer the question: Is there life *before* death? And what kind of life do you want? Allow the certainty of death to shape the way you live your life today. And don't try to handle it by yourself.

Limited time: Don't wait. Act now!

Kids say the funniest things. They say the truest things. My dad took my youngest son, James out for breakfast one morning when he was six-years-old. As they were eating pancakes my dad said to him, "Hey James, I'm taking you to breakfast today. One day you'll take your grandson out for breakfast."

As if he was describing nothing more remarkable than the weather, James said, "Yeah … but you'll be dead." That's it. That's the gist of it. You'll be dead. Stop pretending like your casket is not in the cards. Otherwise, you'll get to the end of the fourth quarter and realize that you missed most of the game.

My uncle's funeral cost $5,000 so far.
We buried him in a rented tuxedo.
—Dave Madden

Your life will not be measured by what you have kept, but by what you contributed.

We'd rather not look at the facts of life … and death. My dad's dad worked on oil rigs. He was a serious guy. He was not a joke teller—except for this one: A preacher asked a Sunday school class of kids, "Raise your hand if you want to go to Heaven." All of the kids raised their hand except for one little boy in the back. The preacher asked the young boy, "Bobby, don't you wanna go to Heaven when you die?" Bobby said, "Oh sure, but I thought you were getting everybody on the bus right now."

AHA! Lesson #10

Life is short.
Have the last laugh.

Questions to ask yourself at a carnival while riding "The Wall of Death":

- Remembering that life is short, how can you make this moment count?
- How can you live more fully today?
- How will you spend today differently in light of the fact that you may not have tomorrow?

- Are you living your life or somebody else's expectations for your life?

- If you were on your deathbed, who would you want to connect with, and what would you want to say to them? Write it/say it to them today!

11

YOUR FAITH IS A JOKE

My karma ran over your dogma.
—Bumper sticker

Before I went full-time as a professional comedy magician, I worked as a youth pastor. I was a junior high director. This is like working with the missing link of evolution. But it was a blast. I bonded with the kids. When I left, I felt bad for the guy who replaced me. On his first Sunday, the kids said to him, "Do a magic trick!"

It's hard to work without an "act." But it's even harder to work without an audience. It cuts way down on the laughter. We are humor beings. When something makes you laugh, you automatically want to make eye contact with the person next to you—even if it's a stranger—because it feels so great to laugh *with* other people. It's all about laughing ... together.

We all need to be part of something that's bigger than ourselves, we need to be part of a community. This is why comedy has much in common with religion and spirituality, and why we're going to talk about those two things now.

Be part of the community

Some people will tell you that all faiths are really the same. I don't think so. There *are* differences, for example:

Protestants don't recognize the Pope as their authority.
Jewish people don't recognize Jesus as the messiah.
Baptists don't recognize each other at the liquor store.

But one important common thread you'll find in people who are thriving in their spiritual journey is this: they see themselves as belonging to a community.

In fact, look at that word "community." *Com* is the root of it. It's where we get great words like comedy, communion, committee—whoops, they're not all great words. But the root is about *com*municating with others who are like-minded. As I just said, comedians can't work without an audience. And *your life doesn't work when you are in* *isolation* and not in community.

Here's where you can get stuck: Don't wait to find the perfect community. You won't find one. In fact, if you do find the perfect temple, church or support group, don't join them. You'll wreck it. I don't belong to any organized religion … I'm a protestant. Actually I'm a spiritual mutt: I grew up in the "Reorganized" LDS faith, became a born-again Christian, then a "Calvinist." I have also been a believing Existentialist, a doubting, prayerful Sunday School teacher with a Catholic grandmother, a devotee of self-help seminars, a close friend with one of the top skeptics in the world, and a student of the 12-step traditions.

All truth is God's truth

Yes, I'm spiritually incorrect, but guess what? There was something to be learned from all of it. All of it was helpful to me as I tried to answer the big questions of life, like ... *How do seedless grapes reproduce?*

About half of the people in the U.S. say they are "spiritual but not religious." The traditional religious person tends to focus on public worship and outward acts of service. The spiritual person, who opts out of organized faith, tends to focus on personal growth and global awareness. When people ask me, "Are you religious or spiritual?" I say, "Yes."

This is because …

A) I like to drive people nuts. When I visit a fast food restaurant and the order-taker asks me, "Will this be for here or to go?" I answer, "To go here." The confusion that sets in is priceless.

B) I want to experience both the purpose and structure of religion, and the "creativity" and connection of spirituality … without feeling like a hypocrite or looking like a flake.

Religion *or* spirituality? Who says it's either or? I say that you can draw from the best of both worlds and enhance your life. I say that I'm spiritualegious. Of course, this may require not only a PS to what you already believe, but also a PPS: A Personal Paradigm Shift. It all starts with seeing that your faith is a joke.

Welcome hypocrites!

"Religious" people can get stuck on the idea that spiritual people are "just a bunch of narcissists." "Spiritual" people can get stuck on the idea that religious people are "just a bunch of hypocrites." It's often true. But lighten up. Your faith is a joke. You're not the only hypocrite.

Relationship expert Barbara De Angelis has been divorced six times. The Beatles sang, "All you need is love" and then started suing each other a few months later. Diet guru Euell Gibbons was dead at 64. *Moral Compass* author Bill Bennett lost millions of dollars playing slots. Believe it or not, even great men and women are hypocrites. Thomas Jefferson said, “All men are created equal,” yet he owned slaves.

The list of hypocrites is a long one. And you and I are on it. Want to know if you are a hypocrite? Check your pulse. If you have one, you are one. The Hypocrite Club. Welcome Aboard! Your community won’t be perfect, but join in anyway.

Rules? I hate rules

When spiritual people complain about religion, they often point to the problem of rules. One of the most-repeated jokes I hear in show biz circles is this one: “Did you hear about the New-age church in California? It has three commandments and seven suggestions.” Even if you think that life is a game (and therefore neither spiritual or religious), remember that even games must have rules. One time I was asked to do a comedy show for a Vacation Bible School. You read that right. Talk about a tough gig. We’re talking little kids. I was asked to explain the 10 Commandments on a level a young child could understand. I’m no rapper, but I came up with this:

The 10 Commandments in rhyme:

Have no other gods, except for me
Do not worship things you make or see
Use God's name just to bless
Take a day off to get some rest
Honor your dad and your mom
Do not murder, that is wrong
When you get married do stay true
Don't take things that don't belong to you
Don't tell lies about someone else
Don't want everything for yourself

The kids *got* it. Why? We love creativity, but our lives also need structure. If we don't have rules, steps, principles, commandments, we don't end up "free." We end up in chaos. There's a problem for us humans with rules, though.

We can't follow rules—even our own. We're human, after all. So we can do one of two things:

1. We can say that we are perfect just as we are and pretend the rules don't apply to us.
2. We can attempt to follow the rules, and when we fail, admit that something is wrong.

The first option is tempting, but it breaks down. It always breaks down. It reminds me of this bumper sticker:

Bad spellers of the world UNTIE!

The perfection problem

Have you noticed that people who tell you that, "You are perfect just as you are," still find the need to convince you of that? But if you were so perfect, wouldn't you know it? And if you are perfect and don't know it, hey … you're not perfect.

It's our brokenness that leads to breakthroughs. You gotta sin to be saved. You gotta hit bottom before you can find recovery. You have to lose yourself before you can find yourself. The hardest person you'll ever have to tell the truth to is yourself. You gotta come clean.

It's not so difficult confessing sins … as long as they're somebody else's. This reminds me of the story of the three pastors who met once a week to encourage each other. These three ministers were growing in trust after meeting together for many months. One day they decided to share their deepest faults and secrets with each other.

The first pastor said, "Well guys, this is embarrassing, but I really struggle with lust. I have never shared this publicly, but I have had several affairs with women at the church." The second minister said, "Well, this is humiliating, and I could even go to jail for this. I have a serious issue with stealing. I have been stealing money from our weekly church offerings." The third pastor was touched by the honesty of his friends. He said, "Guys, thank you for being so transparent. OK … it's my turn. My big sin is that I just can't stop gossiping."

Be careful what you share and who you share it with. But it *is* crucial that you come clean and confess. Share your secrets, sins, and struggles. Be vulnerable. The spiritual recovery groups have much to teach traditional churchgoers in this area. You often can't comfortably go to a church and say, "I don't have things together." In a 12-step type of group, you can confess anything, but you are *not* allowed to say, "I have it all together." You and I don't have it all together … but the sooner we admit that, the better our lives get. Forgiveness is at the root of both religion and spirituality. Gratitude is too.

Don't be like the grandmother who took her five-year-old grandson to the beach. When a giant wave swept him away, she got on her knees and prayed. "Dear Lord, please bring Tommy back to me. I will give my entire life in service to your will." Suddenly another wave brought Tommy safely back to the shore. But instead of being thankful, Tommy's grandmother looked up to heaven and said, "He had a hat."

Breaking hearts … open

Forgiveness, gratitude and joy can transform your life. It goes against the grain of our culture these days to appreciate what you have and to focus on what you can contribute. You have been given many gifts. The way to keep them and enjoy them most is to give them away. Share your gift of teaching. Let other people enjoy your amazing hospitality. Are you a good listener? Well, find someone who needs to be heard, and listen up.

Laughter can instantly change your outlook. When you are at a movie or watching a funny performer at a live event, have you noticed what happens when you laugh? You immediately feel great, and then what? You turn to your partner or friend and there's a look of agreement, "Yes, isn't this wonderful?" And you laugh together.

But don't be like many comedians I know. Don't be miserable making other people laugh but not enjoying life yourself. Don't be like the guilt-inducing cook who makes enough food for everybody but herself. "Oh no, you guys go ahead and eat, I will just enjoy the aroma." Take it deeper than laughter. Let it sink into your heart. I'm not exactly sure why Solomon is called the wisest man who ever lived (he had like 900 wives and girlfriends), but he sure said something profound in the Book of Proverbs: "A cheerful heart is good medicine, but a broken spirit drains your strength."

One often meets his destiny on the road he takes to avoid it.
—Oogway, Kung Fu Panda

I love to make people laugh and think about life, God,

good, evil, and how to lose weight while still eating 17 Ritz crackers and a bowl of sugared cereal at 2:00 am. I wish that some famous spiritual thinker like Emerson or Pascal had said this, but since they didn't, I will tell you: Connect. By all means, *connect, connect, connect.* Learn from other traditions and practices and stay true to your faith. The most important thing is re-connecting with God and with the people around you. I seem to remember someone saying, "Love God and love your neighbor as yourself." Oh yeah, that was Jesus.

AHA! Lesson #11

Experience the purpose of religion *and* the power of spirituality.

Questions to ask yourself when you are not thinking about yourself:

- What community gives you hope?
- What rules should you be following?
- What do you need to come clean about?
- What are you most grateful for?
- What gifts have you been given, and how can you share them?

12

TELL A NEW JOKE

How often do we tell our own life story? And the longer life goes on, the fewer are those around to challenge our account, to remind us that our life is not our life, merely the story we have told about our life. Told to others, but—mainly—to ourselves.
—Julian Barnes

I thought my daughter was going to jump right out of her skin.

Leanna was so über overjoyed that I thought I must be missing something. Had she just been accepted to Harvard? Had she been cast in her own Disney sitcom? She hugged me and thanked me as if I had just handed her the keys to a brand new car. What actually happened: I bought her a cell phone. She had just started 9th grade and suddenly she felt cool, connected, and catapulted into grown-up city. (This was the old days. Now, when babies are born, we remove their umbilical chords and attach smart phones.)

It is pretty amazing when you think about it. Today, you have more computing power in your pocket than was on the first space ship that landed on the moon. The technology is staggering. But how do we use the power? We post photos of our dogs wearing Santa hats. We don't compute that much, we communicate. We speak and write to more people, more quickly, more often.

Cell phones should really be called "tell phones." They have mainly enabled us to tell our stories to each other via talking, texting, emailing, messaging, and posting. No matter how powerful our technology gets, we are still wired to words.

And the words we use are not neutral. They create our experience of life. You attach a meaning to everything in your life the way a clerk at Target uses that label machine gun to attach price tags to products. Boom Boom. Boom. "I'm a loser." "The boss is out to get me." "She's a mean co-worker." "My customers are dumb." You can't stop putting language labels onto everything. You. Just. Can't. Stop. So here's what you need to do to make sure that the words you are using are working for you instead of working you over. Get some new ones.

Thinking: the talking of the soul with itself.
—Plato

Watch your language

Choose your words carefully and on purpose—especially the words you use *inside* your head. As your mom used to say, "Watch your language!" This can be a matter of life or death. We live in our stories like fish live in the sea. Ludwig Wittgenstein was on to something profound when he said, "The limits of my language mean the limits of my world." (I'm happy to tell you that this great thinker also said, "A serious and good philosophical work could be written consisting entirely of jokes.")

> *After twelve years of therapy, my psychiatrist said something that brought tears to my eyes. He said, 'No hablo Ingles.'*
> —Ronnie Shakes

You won't get a different life on the outside until you change your core story on the inside. Your life is an inside joke. Words are the ingredients you use to bake up your stories.

The mixed tape

We use words to attach meaning to our lives. Here's a story that proves how this works: When my divorce was over I was broken up and broke. I was knocked out emotionally and financially. When I started to date again, Barb (my current wife), lived in British Columbia, Canada. I was in California. Despite the distance, I was falling in love. Barb is a super-good woman, and I hung on her every word via phone calls and email exchanges.

Even with the joy Barb brought into my life, one day I was feeling depressed. I was in a funk. But that afternoon, I discovered a package in my mailbox. It was a cassette tape with a music mix on it. It was from Barb.

There was one word written large on the cassette: PARACHUTE. I popped the tape into my car stereo. Wow. I drove for miles and miles so I could listen to the fantastic songs Barb had selected just for me.

PARACHUTE. It was *so* meaningful to me. It blew me away. I thought to myself, *Wow, she really gets what I'm going through. All of these songs—and these lyrics—are really speaking to me.* I was thrilled. I thought: *She's amazing. And she wrote the word PARACHUTE right on the tape. She knows I have been in free fall, and she's telling me that I am going to land safely. Everything's going to be OK.*

After I had listened to the tape about three times, I called Barb and thanked her from the bottom of my heart for such a thoughtful gift. "Thank you for PARACHUTE!"

She said, "Oh good, did you like it? I haven't listened to it. My brother is a D.J. and he made that tape and gave it to me. I'm not really into music, so I sent it to you."

I had to laugh. I was in love, and so in need of a lifeline that I made up a scenario to give myself what I needed. The strange thing was that it worked. I started to feel better about where I was headed in life—and who was going to journey with me. I've since learned to tell Barb's handwriting from my brother-in-law's.

Your life is an inside joke

The words you say are based on what you choose to see. Take the word "crush." You can use it to describe infatuation, destruction, or an orange soda pop. Your life will always be *meaning full*. But you get to choose the way you use words to fill up your cup. Example: If you leave your place of employment, how will you describe that? You could say, "They let me go." Or, "I walked away." Or, "I found a better opportunity." How you see it and then say it will affect you. Things happen, but it's what you make things *mean* that really matters. Words are your binoculars for your outlook on life.

The words you choose can trigger feelings, thoughts, ideas, actions, and even alter the course of your life. Words can be used to heal, and they can be used to harm. Think of a phrase like, "Check enclosed." That's so much better than, "Check your clothes."

Whatever happens in our lives is of little importance. What matters is how we tell the story of what has happened to us.
—Nene Brown

Here's a joke you can tell, even in front of kids, that illustrates the importance of how we interpret words.

A man with a freezer truck is driving some penguins to the zoo. Suddenly his truck breaks down. In a panic, he pulls into a parking lot. He sees a nice-looking family man and says, "Sir, I have to repair this truck. Could you please take these penguins to the zoo?" The man agrees and drives off with the penguins in his mini-van. The next day the truck driver is at the movies. He sees the same man sitting in the theater with the penguins. He says, "Hey, you said you would take the penguins to the zoo." The man says, "Oh I did. We had such a great time. Last night I took them bowling. Today we decided to catch a movie."

I have a crazy hobby. I love to meet authors and ask them to autograph their books to me. The crazy part is that I ask them to personalize words to me and say the exact *opposite* of what their books are about. They look at me funny, but they all do it. A few of my favorites include:

CHARLES T. LEE, the author of *Good Idea. Now What?* wrote, "Adam, I hate to say it but ideas are not your thing."

TIM PAULSON, the author of *Love and Grow Rich* wrote to me, "Adam, I can't stand you."

DAVID STOOP, the author of *Self-Talk: Key to Personal Growth* wrote, "Adam, you're an idiot."

That last one is my favorite. My family and friends are shocked when they open up my books and see these handwritten notes and the author signatures. They can't believe I would want to read that stuff. But these contradictory comments make me laugh. They remind me that my life is a joke. David Stoop is right. What we say to ourselves *is* the key to personal growth. You can nod your head in agreement. But do you say hateful things to yourself? You talk to yourself all day long. *You must control that conversation.* The stories you tell are like "inside jokes." This inner dialogue is the soundtrack to the movie of your life. How do you like it? Your life is a few outer experiences and a thousand inner explanations.

Imagine this: What if your brain was a PA system and everybody around you could hear the way you talk to and about yourself. Within a 30-second time frame they might hear you say, "I am a dunce. I've done it again. It's because I'm fat. I'm losing my memory. I'm going to look like such a fool at this party." They would think you were crazy. But then, when you speak to someone else, your language is quickly transformed: "Oh, hello. It's so great to see you. Yes, I'm doing fine. How are you?" Change the language of your life, and change your life. Which person would you rather be? If you dislike the way you speak to yourself, it may be time to introduce your inner child to your outer adult.

This is your brain on stories

It's astonishing what can get stuck on your brain. It reminds me of the man who goes in to see the psychiatrist. The man has a colorful parrot on top of his head. The psychiatrist says, "Hello, how can I help you?" The parrot says, "Can you get this guy off my foot?"

The words you use always flow from your point of view.

And the dialogue in your head is nonstop. Have you noticed that you argue with yourself? Think about *that*. It is like the woman who goes to the doctor. The doctor asks her, "How are you feeling?"

She says, "I ate something that doesn't agree with me."

And immediately a little voice from her stomach says, "No you haven't!"

It takes serious effort to speak to yourself with integrity. And that word, integrity, is about alignment and becoming whole, not perfect.

> *We negotiate our way through life by the guidance of our stories.*
> —Loyal Rue

Your mind is a stage full of fictional characters all talking to each other ... and you. But remember: You don't have to believe everything you think. Your life is a joke. Stop telling the stale one that just isn't funny. Don't be like the foolish man who kept smashing his head against a brick wall over and over. When he was asked, "Why do you keep doing that?" he answered, "Because it feels so good when I stop!"

If I've said it once ...

I have a comedian friend who is in his fifties now. He has told me the same word-for-word story about his life for thirty years—a sad tale about how another performer ripped him off. *Dude, get a new story, get a new life.* And since our language = our lives, we need to see our words in a whole new way. We have to face the fact that our facts are mostly fiction. (Read that sentence again). We have repeated them so often, we have convinced ourselves that these made-up stories are true. We need to go back and learn words that will empower us. But not everybody wants to go back to school.

A dad told his son, "Son, you better wake up. You need to get to school."

His son answered, "Dad, I don't want to go to school."

His dad said, "And why is that?"

The son answered, "There are three reasons, Dad. One, I'm so tired of it. Two, it feels like I've been going there forever. And three, the kids all make fun of me."

His dad says, "I'll give you three reasons why you have to go. One, you are supposed to be there. Two, you are forty-five-years old. Three, you are the principal!"

Re-educating yourself means re-writing some of the old core stories of your life. And it starts—it always starts—with your *premise*. You and I think that we are making new and original statements. But our words pour out of our prior world view. Your outlook on life is embedded with rules, rituals, and rewards. This is a fascinating thing. We create our world view, and then we live in a world we never realize we have made!

As a man thinks in his heart, so he is.
—Proverb of Solomon

Think about what hurts

Don't confuse what feels normal with what is true. You've heard that your brain is like a computer. Well, get a new screen saver. Sometimes you need to refresh your browser. But get this: Before you actually will change your point of view, something important has to be at risk. Take my advice. (I'm not using it).

Reexamine your main "signature" stories and drop the ones that are no longer serving you. Before you will change those stories that you are living from, you'll need a strong dose of motivation. Hint: Think about what hurts. Think about what hurts real bad.

As a comedian, it's not easy for me when I make changes

to my "act." But I have to do it to reach new audiences and have new experiences. The problem is that I have been delivering many of the same jokes and stories the same way for so long, I begin to think there's only one way to tell them. But something happens when I try out new material: I get a different reaction. I might get no laughs. I might get huge laughs. But I get something new. You can too.

If you're not writing a new story for your life, you may be living someone else's story for you. That "someone" might be the old you still dictating what you should think, say, and do.

A friend of mine has a trophy wife.
Apparently, it wasn't first place.
—Steven Wright

Words are not only weapons. They are drugs. Make sure you know what you are taking. I have pointed out that we are by nature meaning-attachers. We label everything. Be sure to carefully *read the labels*. Your happiness, your success, your health, your relationships, are all affected by the words that you have swallowed and are now part of your belief system. Think I'm overstating this? Rudyard Kipling was a master storyteller (*Jungle Book, The Man Who Would Be King*). Here's what he had to say: "Words are, of course, the most powerful drug used by mankind."

I've seen humorous words instantly lift someone out of sadness. I've also seen humor hurt people. As Steve Martin said, "Comedy is not pretty." It depends on the words that are used and how they are used. Imagine telling a scared child, "Mommy's *gone*." Terror. But replace one word, and that child's perspective changes in an instant: "Mommy's *here*."

According to "Verbal First Aid" experts Judith Acosta and Judith Simon Prager, "When people are in a medical emergency, or a crisis caused by illness or emotion, they already know something terrible has happened. The good news is that the terrible thing has *already happened* … there is one *magic sentence* that opens the door to rapport in acute situations: *The worst is over.* The effect that one little sentence has on the chemical processes of the body can be profound." (From *The Worst Is Over* by Judith Acosta and Judith Simon Prager). What words can you say goodbye to in order to make room for language you can live with?

We've been talking a lot about the words you think and say. But it's also critical that you *listen* to worthwhile words. Sometimes you have to listen carefully before the message you need to hear really sinks in.

Listen deeply to the language that will help you find your way home. And remember, you will always use words to interpret what happens to you. Choose wise words. You are a meaning maker. That's a good thing. Your life is a joke. Tell a good one.

The meaning of life ... com

So, how did I finally get the meaning of life? In the introduction to this book, I told you that out of all of the billions of people on earth, the "The Meaning of Life" was given to *me*. Here's what happened. I was up late one night. Like 2:00 am. I thought to myself, *Hey, I wonder who has the website for TheMeaningofLife.com?* I discovered that a woman in Florida named Melanie Shannon was using it to share nature photos and inspiring poems. I sent her an email saying hello and congratulating her on owning this "ultimate" domain name. After a few email exchanges, she knew that looking for answers to life's big questions was my passion. She said, "Adam, I want you to have TheMeaningofLife.com. It's my gift to you."

That's what it means. The meaning of life, like the domain, is a gift. I thought it was something I had to get, but it is actually something I was given.

Dear Reader, I wrote a poem to conclude our time together. It's called *Your Life is a Joke*. Looking for feedback, I read it to my youngest daughter, Katie. She listened to the poem and said. "Dad, I like it … except for everything." That made me laugh. I rewrote the poem. And I remembered that *I can rewrite the story of my life and tell it in a new way.* So can you.

Here is the new version:

YOUR LIFE IS A JOKE
A poem by Adam Christing

I was sad when I realized my life is a joke
Year after year I felt emotionally broke
If my life was a test, I got a "D" on the quiz
I told my same old story, "It is what it is"
But then, an "AHA" moment, it felt like a sign ...
Change your setup to change your punch line
Turns out, you're the writer, so quick, grab a pen
Write a better beginning and start over again
You can tell a new story. Feel free. Go for broke
You'll be glad you discovered your life is a joke

AHA! Lesson #12

Change your story, change your life.

Questions to ask yourself to tell a better joke about your life:

- What one word best describes your life now?
- What word or phrase do you want to use to describe your life?

- What is the "signature" story of your life? Would you like to change it?
- What are you saying to and about yourself?
- Can you think of a magical sentence that will reframe your perspective and transform your life story?
- How could your life change by telling your story in a new way (with a new set-up and punch line)?

BONUS SECTION:
25 clean jokes *you* can tell
and some tips for how to tell them

1) I called the "PSYCHIC HOTLINE." When the lady said, "Who's calling?" I said, "You tell me!"

2) A SKELETON walks into a bar. The bartender says, "What'll you have?" The skeleton says, "Give me a pitcher of beer and a mop."

3) A man bursts into a doctor's office and says, "Doctor you've got to help me, I THINK I'M A MOTH. The doctor says, "Well, I can't help you. I'm a general M.D. I'm not a psychiatrist. Why did you come to my office?" The man shrugs and says, "Your light was on."

4) THE ECONOMY is rough. My wife and I sat our kids on the couch the other night. We just told them straight up, "We're going to have to let one of you go."

5) THE ICE FISHERMAN had a few too many beers when he went out to fish one night. He dug a hole in the ice and looked down. He heard a voice, "There are no fish down there." He moved about 20 feet. He dug another hole, but just as he was ready to throw his line in, he heard the voice again. "There are no fish down there." So he moved about 50 feet away. He dug another hole. He looked down and heard that booming voice again. "THERE ARE NO FISH DOWN THERE." The fisherman looked up, "God, is that you?" And the loud voice said, "No, this is the manager of the ice rink. Go home!"

Tips for telling: When you speak the "God, is that you?" line, do it with reverence—like the guy is really in awe.

6) A LITTLE BOY never speaks a single word to anybody. His parents are very worried about him. Finally, one day when he is six-years-old the family is at the dinner table and the boy blurts out, "Mom, these tacos are terrible. I hate them!" His parents are thrilled to hear him speak. His mom says, "Honey, we have been waiting for years to hear you say something. Why haven't you spoken until now?" The little boy says, "Well, up until now everything was okay."

7) A MARRIAGE COUNSELOR is talking to a 92-year-old wife and her 94-year-old husband. They are miserable and want to get a divorce. The counselor says, "But you two have been married for 70 years. Has some-

thing suddenly changed?" The husband says, "Nope, I have been sick of her for years." The elderly wife says, "I never did like him. It's over. I want out." The counselor says, "All these years together! Why do you want to get a divorce now?" The old man says, "Well, we wanted to wait until the kids were dead."

8) The OWNER OF A MOVIE THEATER died. His wife sent out a mass email to family and friends. It said: "Larry's funeral will be held on Thursday at 2:30, 4:10, 6:20 and 8:45.

9) A COP pulls over a husband and wife who are speeding. The cop tells the man, "Sir, you were speeding." The wife says, "Honey, I told you to slow down!" The husband tells her to be quiet. The cop says, "Sir, you also made an illegal U-turn a mile back." The man's wife says, "Yes, he sure did." The man tells his wife, "Will you shut up?" The cop tells the man, "And I notice, Sir, that your registration tags are expired." The wife says, "You didn't take care of that last month?" The husband says to his wife, "Keep your mouth shut!" Finally the cop says to the woman, "Is your husband always this rude to you?" And she says, "No officer, only when he's drunk."

10) A man was driving on a back road to look at some property. He suddenly saw a CHICKEN racing past him at over 60 miles an hour. The man noticed that the chicken had

three legs. He went down the side road and saw a barn. He saw a farmer there and asked him, "Did you see a chicken go by here?" The farmer says, "Yep." The man says, "Did it have three legs?" And the farmer says, "Yep. That's how I breed them." The man says, "You do? How come?" And the farmer says, "Well I just love the drumstick. And my wife prefers the drumstick. And our son likes the drumstick best. We got tired of fighting over it. So I've been breeding three-legged chickens." And the driver says, "Well, how do they taste?" The farmer says, "I don't know. I haven't been able to catch one yet."

11) A CHRISTMAS SHOPPER is frantically trying to get his last-minute shopping done in time for Christmas. He's driving all around the mall desperately trying to find a parking space. He's about to give up hope. He says a prayer: "Lord, if you will help me find a parking spot, I promise to go to church every Sunday, I will help the poor, and I will become a better husband." Instantly he sees a parking space open up. He prays again, "Oh, never mind, Lord. I found one."

12) Here's one thing you'll never hear at a CATHOLIC SCHOOL: "So … what are you wearing tomorrow?"

13) A GOLFER is bragging to his buddy about his special purple golf ball. He says, "This ball is the greatest golf ball

ever invented. You can't ever lose it. At night it glows in the dark. If you hit it into the water, it floats up to the surface. If you hit the ball out into the rough, it has an alarm inside and you can hear it beeping really loud. The man's buddy says, "Wow. That is incredible. Where did you get it?" The golfer says, "Oh, I found it."

Tips for telling: When telling this punch line, do it very casually, in an off-hand way.

14) A TOURIST landed in Chicago and walked up to the car rental booth. "How long will it take to get from here to Orlando?" he asked. The rental agent said, "Just a minute, Sir." The man (walking away) said, "Thanks a lot."

15) A man and his wife were flying to HAWAII. They were arguing about how you pronounce the word *Hawaii.* The man says, "Honey, everybody knows it's Ha-why-ee." His wife kept challenging him, "No, it's actually Ha-vie-ee." They kept arguing. "Ha-why-ee." "No, it's Ha-vie-ee." Finally, the woman tapped the shoulder of the old man seated in front of them. "Excuse me, sir, my husband and I can't agree. How do you pronounce the name of the island where we're going?" The man says, "Oh, that's easy. It's Ha-vie-ee." The woman gloats to her husband, "See I told you!" She says to the man, "Thank you for settling that, sir." And the old man says, "You're vel-come."

16) What's the difference between a MUSICIAN AND A PIZZA? A pizza can feed a family of four.

17) I'M WORRIED about my health. My doctor called and said, "Your test results are back, and I need to tell you that you have ten … " I interrupted him. "Ten what? Ten years? Ten months? Ten weeks!" He said, "NINE, EIGHT, SEVEN, SIX … "

18) My brother is an ADDICT. He is currently hooked on drinking brake fluid. He says he can stop any time.

19) Here's a brilliant thing to say when you get caught SLEEPING AT WORK: "I'm so sorry—they told me at the blood bank that this might happen."

20) How many psychotherapists does it take to CHANGE A LIGHT BULB? One. But the light bulb has to *want* to be changed.

21) How many COMPUTER SUPPORT TECHS does it take to change a light bulb? Answer: "Have you tried switching it off and on again?"

22) A man pounds on his PSYCHOTHERAPIST'S door. She lets him in and he says excitedly, "Thanks for seeing me. I think I've had a breakthrough." His therapist is

happy to hear this and says, "That sounds wonderful. What happened?" The man says, "It was a dream I had last night. I was talking to my mom in the dream and suddenly my mom turned into *you*. So, when I woke up this morning, I threw some clothes on, grabbed a diet Coke and a cinnamon roll and rushed over here to your office." The psychotherapist says, "A diet Coke and a cinnamon roll? That's not *breakfast!*"

23) A man goes to his support group meeting and HE STINKS. The other member's of the group can hardly stand sitting anywhere near him. Finally, when it's his turn to share he says, "Hi everybody. My problem is I can never get a woman to go out with me on a date. They all say no." One of the women in the group speaks up, "Well, I know what it is. Sorry, but you reek. You smell terrible." The man says, "Oh, that's because I work with a circus, and it's my job to follow the elephants around and clean up their droppings. Every day the stink just sticks to me." The woman says, "Well, why don't you get a different job?" The man says, "Are you kidding me? And give up show business?"

24) A man walks into a bar. The bartender says, "Hey there. I've got a great new joke about GOVERNMENT WORKERS. Wanna hear it?" The man says, "Hey, hold on. I work for the government." The bartender says, "No problem. I'll tell it really, really slow."

25) Bob was way OUT OF SHAPE. He was about 100 pounds overweight. When he turned 50 he decided to finally get healthy. He joined a gym. He started riding a bike to work. He stopped eating red meat. He cut out all sweets, and drank only water. It worked. Bob lost all his extra weight. He slimmed down. He got tan. And he bought all new clothes. Bob got a cool haircut to celebrate his new look. He walked out of the hair salon and was immediately run over by a truck and died instantly. When he got to Heaven he said, "I worked so hard, God. How could you have done that to me?" God said, "Sorry, Bob. I didn't recognize you."

5 Tips for better joke telling

Let your set-up sink in for your listeners before you tell the rest of the story. Let them know who it's about.

Don't just tell it ... live it. The more you invest (with your voice, your movements, your commitment to the story), the better.

Punch up your punch lines. Pause before the final line. And hit them hard with the surprise ending.

Have fun, but keep a straight face. The straighter you tell a joke—like it really happened—the funnier it will be.

Wait for them to laugh. Don't laugh at your own joke. That's what you want your audience to do.

ACKNOWLEDGMENTS

Heartfelt love and thanks go to my wife and family: Barb, Leanna & Steamer, Randy, Katie, James, Mom & Dad, John & Dorothy, Diana & Louis, Shelly & Mark, Mike & Catrina. This book would not have been possible without my awesome wife and incredible family.

I could not get along without my friends: Michael Levine, David O'Shaughnessy, Nick Arnette, Brian Godawa, Greg Bennick, Chris & Dolly Blackmore, Scott Grossberg, Ruben Padilla, Tim Fillmore, Lenda Travis, Dean White, The Rummell Family, The Leith Family, Kermit & Jennifer Jones, Les Mazon, Les Duncan, Les Moore, Chris Dorman, Phil Liberatore, Corey Ford, Mark Joseph, David Boufford, David Di Sabatino, Brian Keith Voiles (and McKay!), Bob Korljan, Sean Bott, Karen Armstrong, Mark Matteson, Karen Millard, Jay & Sally Mincks, Doug Wicks, Luke Tai, Ken Felig, Ron Forseth, Kim Levings, Mike Riggs, Bill Ankerberg, Paul Green, Sandy Chanley, Rich & Eileen Blagden, Paul Rosenow, Trinity Reprographics, The Seed Company, WACC, High Desert Church, Viasystems, Insperity, Steve Bridges (you are missed).

A partial list of my wonderful partners in performance: Paul "Book'em" Brown, Bob & Kim Westfall, Ryan & Sarah Richards (but not their dog), Tiffany Vazquez, Mike Toupin, Corey Ponder, Chris McDonald, Rob Murray, Cary Trivanovich, John Hakel, Errin Hogan, Amanda Renfrew, Cheri Najor, Don Magnoli, Patti Allen, Missy Weld, Dee Dawson, The State of Maine, Pete McLeod, Dana Daniels, Chris Yim, BigSpeak, Robert Channing, Philly Mendelson, T. Faye Griffin, Scott & Yoney Wood, Chipper Lowell, Robert Strong, Dystel & Goderich Literary Management. Special thanks to Lisa Marie Franco.

Mentors: Frank Rodriguez (who taught me to mark in books), Dr. Todd V. Lewis, Richard Machowicz, Brian Tracy, Jay Abraham, Gary & Carol Richmond, The Ernest Becker Foundation, Don Bishop, Robert Zimmerman.

LBBC and my secret success group, I can't share the names of the members or they will assassinate me. But their initials are: S, R, T, D and L.

My lifelong Creek Park friends and an assortment of basketball buddies: Brian, Tammye, Steve, Greg, Kim, Clowie, Cindy, Manoj, Anju, Cotty, Nancy, Big Dave, Rob, Wiley, "The Printer," and more … but not Ross (unless he's on my team.)

This book became possible because of friends and family who supported my Kickstarter campaign. (The complete list can be found at YourLifeIsAJoke.com.) Special thanks to: Drew Dickens, William King, Caring Voice Coalition, Kevin Finn, Cecile Kaiser and Scott Grossberg.

Huge thanks to the following people who made this book bigger and far better: Evan Davis, who reminded me that I was not writing the Bible, Robert G. Lee pumped up the humor and Todd Brabender (Spread TheNewsPR.com).

Mega thanks to Lisa Knight, the star of "Breaking Good" and the fastest and best designer on the planet. Check out DesignsDoneNow.com when you need a great design for just about anything.

Special recognition goes to my incredible book coach and editor, the "cheerleader with a whip," Jennie Nash. When you are ready to create *your* book, do yourself a favor and visit JennieNash.com.

ABOUT THE AUTHOR

ADAM CHRISTING is the founder of CleanComedians.com. He earned a degree in public speaking from Biola University and has been named to the university's alumni "Hall of Fame." At age 17, he became a member of the world famous Magic Castle in Hollywood. Adam studied comedy with Sandy Holt of *Second City* and is a popular keynote speaker, emcee, and comedy-magician. He has been ranked among the top five after-dinner speakers in the United States. He is the co-writer and co-director of the comedy "mockumentary" called *Change Your Life!* (ChangeYourLifeTheMovie.com).

For more information visit: AdamChristing.com. Email the author at adam@adamchristing.com.